What Are They Saying About Biblical Archaeology?

Leslie J. Hoppe, O.F.M.

Illustrations by Frank Sabatté, C.S.P.

PAULIST PRESS
New York/Ramsey

Library of Congress
Catalog Card Number: 83-63110

ISBN: 0-8091-2613-3

Published by Paulist Press
545 Island Road, Ramsey, N.J. 07446

Printed and bound in the
United States of America

Contents

Introduction   1

1 Archaeology—Use and Abuse   3

2 The Excavation Project—From Start to Finish   13

3 Ebla—Controversy and Promise   34

4 Jerusalem—David's City   45

5 Capernaum—The City of Jesus   58

6 Nabratein and Its Ark   79

7 The Future of Biblical Archaeology   90

Bibliography   101

Introduction

Biblical archaeology is experiencing rapid growth on two fronts. First of all the pace of excavation has quickened very much in the last fifteen years. Along with this rush of activity in the field, there has been a significant discussion within the discipline regarding a variety of theoretical issues. This book tries to introduce the reader to some developments on both fronts. The first two chapters plus the last one deal with some of these theoretical issues and what gave rise to them. More than anything else it has been the increasing sophistication of archaeological techniques which has caused archaeologists to reconsider what direction their discipline ought to take. In addition, the question of the relationship between archaeology and biblical studies, which has always been a controverted issue, looms large in these theoretical discussions. Chapters 3 through 6 describe four excavation projects which are still in progress or have just been completed. Each project, which comes from a different archaeological period, illustrates some of the problems excavators face today, the methods of excavation they employ and the accomplishments they have made. Each chapter concludes with a bibliography that can be used to gain more information on the matter presented in the respective chapters.

The enterprise of biblical archaeology is about one hundred and fifty years old. What began with a solitary scholar riding through Palestine on a donkey in order to survey biblical sites continues today with teams of scholars still in the field but joined by colleagues in laboratories analyzing artifacts and studying computer printouts. To say that biblical archaeology has undergone a series of revolutionary changes in the last one hundred and fifty years is an understatement. The aim of this book is to help the reader appreciate what biblical archaeologists are doing and saying as they prepare to make another important leap forward.

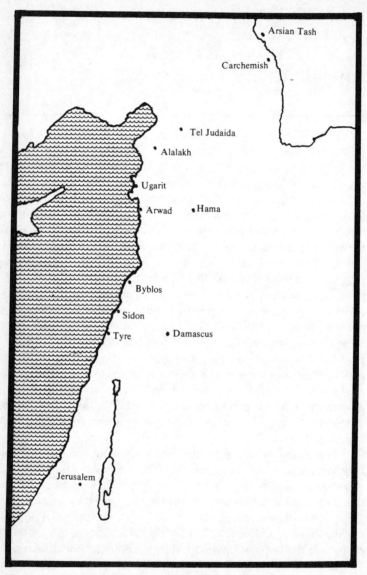

The Major Archaeological Sites of Syria

1
Archaeology—Use and Abuse

The definitions of archaeology vary. Perhaps the most useful is one which designates archaeology as the study of the material remains of antiquity as opposed to its literary remains. Sometimes in the course of excavations literary remains are found. These may range from a few letters scratched on a potsherd, to inscriptions chiseled on monuments, to collections of scrolls such as found at Qumran. These written materials are handed over to experts in epigraphy, paleography and philology who may not be archaeologists. Archaeology is concerned with material remains from the largest structures to the smallest artifacts. Any object which gives evidence of human activity is fair game for the archaeologist—whether these objects be coin hoards which may testify to the thrift of the ancients or some parched bones which may be the remnants of a meal consumed long ago. Archaeology uncovers these objects, identifies them, reconstructs where possible and necessary and then classifies them. Once these preliminary tasks have been completed, the more difficult begin: the artifacts are compared with examples from similar cultures, they are arranged in a chronological sequence and they are related to previously known information about antiquity. All this is done in order to reconstruct life in the ancient world, to trace the development of the people who left these remains behind, and to help define the various types of human responses to different situations. Archaeology fills a void where literary sources are insufficient or non-existent. Where there are literary sources such as the Bible, archaeology helps to put these into a living context.

Unfortunately archaeology can and has been used for purposes other than those which properly belong to it. For archaeology to be of any benefit the limitations on its use need to be understood. What can archaeology do and what can archaeology not do?

Archaeology as Treasure Hunting

In its infancy, archaeology was sometimes little more than treasure hunting to secure "finds" for public or private collections in Europe and America. Ancient sites were quite literally plundered for the benefit of Western museums. The little sophistication there was in the techniques of excavating and recording was often ignored in the rush to make some spectacular find. Fortunately this does not happen on any large scale today. Governments are very careful to oversee all archaeological expeditions in order to insure that the work will be done under the supervision of competent archaeologists who will employ the state of the art techniques in their work. All artifacts found in the course of excavation are the property of the government, and rightly so, since these artifacts are part of its national cultural treasure. Occasionally such treasure hunting still occurs on a small scale. For example, laborers at sites have been known to pilfer what they consider to be valuable and especially salable artifacts such as coins. With the invention of metal detectors it has become easy for amateurs to do their own treasure hunting. Naturally governments do not look kindly on such activities.

Archaeology and Politics

It should not be surprising that biblical archaeology gets caught up in the tangled web of Middle Eastern politics so that archaeology has to serve political purposes—quite obviously an end which is incompatible with archaeology's true purposes. Licenses for excavations have become political footballs. Certain archaeologists have become *personae non gratae* in some countries simply because they have been engaged in projects in other countries. Certain types of projects are either encouraged or discouraged because they will support or undercut "historical" arguments used to legitimate territorial claims. Archaeology can become an expression of nationalism and foreign policy. Of course, archaeology ought never to be brought into the arena of contemporary political conflicts though archaeologists have to deal with this reality.

Archaeology and the Bible

Some people seek to use archaeology as a means to demonstrate the historicity of the Bible. Such people are generally fundamentalist Christians whose theological principles require that the Bible be proven to be historically accurate. Some have carried this concern to such an extreme that attempts have been made to find Noah's ark, the ark of the covenant and Moses' tomb. Occasionally the press will report the extravagant claims of those who claim to have found Noah's ark and the like, but no scientific report is even made of such "discoveries"—for obvious reasons.

Besides these clearly misguided attempts by biblical fundamentalists, there are still many reputable people who still look to archaeology as a means to undergird the historical accuracy of the Bible as if such historical precision guarantees the religious truth made by the biblical text. Such efforts may be well intentioned but they are ultimately of limited value. One example may clarify the situation. Josephus was a first century A.D. Jewish historian whose works are basically an *apologia* for Judaism directed at a Greco-Roman audience. This patently ideological purpose has led historians to doubt the reliability of Josephus in providing historical detail. Archaeology has served to rehabilitate Josephus' reputation as an historian. Despite a new confidence in the accuracy of some of Josephus' data, the contemporary reader still has to deal with the ancient author's perspectives and historical theses which need to be evaluated apart from the issue of his now recognized reliability in terms of historical detail.

In a similar fashion, the historical reliability of the Book of Joshua is one thing; its theological affirmations are quite another. While Joshua reflects some historical data, its historical value is quite limited. The "facts" surrounding Israel's acquisition of her land serve as the backdrop for the drama of Israel's life with God. Like scenery these facts are meant to be suggestive rather than precise representations. It is a mistake to focus on the scenery when the real action takes place at center stage—the interaction between God and Israel. The simplicity and complexity of this relationship—not the communication of historical data—are what occupied the author of Joshua. Unfortunately some people maintain that one goal of archaeology is to verify the historical data provided by the Bible. But archaeology does not "prove" the Bible; it only proves one's interpretation of the Bible—an interpretation often formulated apart from any archaeological data. The truth of the Bible as a religious book cannot be proven or disproven by archaeology. The Bible's message is to be accepted by faith. Even what some people call Israel's "sacred history" is beyond the pale of archaeology. This sacred history is after all a religious interpretation of events. This interpretation cannot be confirmed or denied by the archaeologist's trowel. The most archaeology can do is to help establish some of the facts which the Bible has employed in its interpretations of Israel's history.

There is a great temptation to minimize archeological discoveries which undercut one's approach to the historical reliability of the Bible. There is also the danger of producing an artificial harmony between texts and archaeological work by reading too much from the material excavated. One needs to remember that most of the archaeological data that exist are still below the ground. There is always the possibility that new discoveries and new techniques will make what appears to be the "assured results" of archaeological work quite out of date.

The best example of the problems in relating the Bible to archaeology centers around the so-called conquest, i.e., the biblical acount of how ancient Israel acquired the land which was to be the scene of its subsequent history. The Book of Joshua describes this process as the result of a military campaign by a united Israel under the leadership of Joshua. This campaign consisted of a thrust into central Canaan followed by forays into the south and the north. Once these were complete, the land was divided among the Israelite tribes. Archaeologists have excavated a number of sites associated with the battles fought by Joshua.

Kathleen Kenyon who excavated Jericho concluded that there was no wall there during the period usually associated with the Israelite conquest (the Late Bronze Age III: 1300–1200 B.C.). She did observe the remnants of a wall from the Middle Bronze Age (2200–1550 B.C.), which may have been the wall the biblical author had in mind when describing the Israelite takeover of Jericho (Joshua 6). Now Kenyon excavated only a small portion of Jericho. At some later date there may be discoveries at Jericho which will cause a re-examination of this whole issue.

According to the Bible Joshua turned to Ai after the defeat of Jericho (Joshua 8). Judith Marquet-Krauser and Joseph Callaway have found absolutely no evidence whatsoever of a Late Bronze Age occupation at Ai. The site was in ruins centuries before the Israelites came to Canaan. Though further excavation may turn up something later, extensive work up to now has not unearthed even a single Late Bronze Age potsherd. In this case there is a clear difference between the biblical tradition and archaeological excavation.

The excavation at Hazor under Yigael Yadin has offered no contradiction to the biblical story of Hazor's fall before Joshua's forces (Jos 11). Yadin has shown that Hazor went through a violent destruction during the Late Bronze Age. But even here the evidence is ambiguous. Was this destruction caused by the invading Israelites as the Bible claims, or was it caused by some other group? After all, the Late Bronze Age was one of considerable turmoil in Canaan. The site itself provides no means of identifying those who were responsible for its destruction. Even this apparent "confirmation" of the biblical text by archaeology is ambiguous to some extent.

Though the archaeological evidence may be difficult to interpret at times, this does not mean that archaeology cannot help illuminate biblical texts. Often difficult texts are made much clearer as a result of archaeological excavations. The project studying David's city outside the present Old City of Jerusalem has clarified the meaning of the word *millo* (2 Sam 5:9; 1 Kgs 9:15). Most English translations simply transliterate this Hebrew word which means "filling." Excavations have revealed the existence of a large stepped-stone structure which probably buttressed a large building, perhaps a citadel. Such support would be necessary for any large building erected on the steep slopes of David's Jerusalem. Of course, such a structure would need to be carefully maintained to compensate for the ravages of erosion, torrential rain and earthquake.

Archaeology can also serve to confirm the reliability of certain types of information provided by the text. For example, Nathanael implies that Nazareth was an unimportant village (Jn 1:46). Excavations at Nazareth have confirmed Nathanael's judgment. The Book of Kings describes the building activities of Solomon at the cities of Gezer, Megiddo and Hazor (1 Kgs 9:15). Each of these cities shows evidence of the extent of Solomon's building projects.

Finally archaeology can provide information which the ancient texts simply do not have. This is especially true of excavations of synagogues whose artifacts come from a period after the major literary sources dealing with synagogues were written. It would be foolish to try to draw some conclusions about Palestinian Judaism solely on the basis of literary records. There is just too much archaeological data to be ignored.

Archaeology Reveals Antiquity

Though it is important to be aware of the limitations of archaeology, it is equally important to realize that archaeology is an invaluable tool in understanding antiquity. Texts alone are not the only available means to deal with the questions that naturally arise in the study of ancient Israel, early Judaism and early Christianity. Obviously archaeology is not some kind of a nostrum which will solve every difficulty, but the use of ancient texts together with the results of archaeological investigation will contribute to the clarification of many problems of interpretation.

While the intersection of textual evidence and archaeological work is the goal of many biblical archaeologists, some suggest that it is now necessary for archaeology to become a discipline which is independent of any connection with the Bible. The archaeologist is neither an exegete nor an historian. The archaeologist is a specialist in the recovery, classification and description of the material remains of antiquity. Such a view is the result of a profound shift in the self-concept of archaeologists who feel ill at ease with the way archaeology has been used in biblical scholarship. To some extent, this feeling is well founded. The results of archaeological excavation dictate the kind of information that can be provided to the historian and exegete. But what assurance can the archaeologists give that the data they provide are such that valid generalizations can be drawn from them? After all, archaeology can uncover only what has survived, and what has survived and been discovered is the result of sheer accident. Secondly, interpreters sift through this evidence in terms of their own intellectual and sometimes theological background which is conditioned by contemporary social, cultural and religious concerns—not by those of antiquity. To deal with this situation honestly some archaeologists would limit their work to the material aspects of culture and ignore the non-material components of the culture.

In such a perspective the main goals of archaeology become the definition of basic types of structures and artifacts, the search for similarities in form, function, association and developmental sequences among particular types and the development of principles which can guide the correlation of the preceding data. If these are the only goals of biblical archaeology, one can legitimately ask about the purpose of expending a great amount of time, talent and money to sort out pottery types of Palestine. While the move to strengthen the quality of archaeology's analytical task is commendable and necessary, it does not follow that archaeologists ought to abandon all interest in the historical event, the development of institutions and the interrelationships among the different aspects of human society. One task of the archaeologist is to contribute to knowledge about the social institutions, attitudes and beliefs of antiquity. Of course, these cannot be quantified. They cannot be inferred from artifacts alone. They are, however, legitimate concerns for the archaeologists to keep in mind during the course of excavation and later during the interpretation of data. It is the responsibility of archaeologists to keep reminding historians and exegetes of the relative value of the data they provide.

What can archaeology contribute to our knowledge of antiquity? The contribution archaeology can make depends in a large measure on the archaeologists' willingness to overcome their hesitancy to deal with the non-material aspects of culture. It is intellectually dishonest to act as if artifacts functioned in any society independently of non-material variables such as politics, religion, social values, technological skills, kinship and ethnic identity. One goal of archaeology should be the illumination of the process of social and cultural change as it is revealed in the material remains of antiquity. If this goal is to be achieved in a convincing way, archaeologists will have to depend upon other disciplines such as sociology, anthropology, economics and quantitative analysis to provide them not only with the interpretive tools but also with the theoretical underpinning necessary to make valid observations about an ancient society. This goes beyond simple description and cataloguing of artifacts at which archaeologists have become masters.

Archaeologists ought to be concerned about giving *meaning* to the data they have discovered and recorded. This involves a concerted effort to link archaeological data with human behavior. Archaeologists will provide the information necessary to formulate, test and confirm hypotheses regarding how patterns of human behavior change or remain the same. In other words, the goal of archaeology is not simply to describe and classify artifacts but to describe a living society and what held it together or tore it apart—on the basis of what that society has left behind.

Archaeology and Texts

While it is important that archaeology not ignore its relationship to the Bible, the concerns of those who want archaeology to strike its own course independently of biblical interpretation are valid. Clearly archaeology's purpose is not to "prove" the Bible. Even the overriding objective of some biblical archaeologists to have their science provide an historical foundation for biblical narratives such as those about the conquest need to be questioned. The problem of the relationship between the Bible and archaeology is not solved simply by correlating archaeological and literary evidence. Archaeology can be used to determine whether and to what extent the Bible itself has any value for historical reconstruction. Until recently it seemed as though the contribution of archaeology to understanding the world of ancient Israel, early Judaism and early Christianity was minimal due to the quantity and quality of the available written sources. Archaeology was an interesting but ultimately unnecessary diversion for the biblical scholar. Now it is apparent that archaeology can raise questions that are either peripheral or are ignored in the biblical material.

A striking example is provided by the discoveries at Kuntillet Ajrud, a remote site in southern Judah. At this site, which its excavator Zeev Meshel considers to have been a religious center, two pithoi (singular: pithos; large storage jar) were found which bore inscriptions and drawings. One of the inscriptions reads: "May you be blessed by Yahweh and his Asherah." (Asherah is a female deity of Canaan.) Below this inscription is a drawing of three figures, two of which are assumed by Meshel to represent Yahweh and his consort Asherah. It is tempting to find a connection between the inscription and the drawing, though the nature of their relationship is not absolutely clear. In any case, archaeology has opened up for study and discussion an issue never raised by the biblical text: Did ancient Israel, at one point in its religious quest, believe that Yahweh had a consort?

Besides referring to a female deity, the word "Asherah" can also refer to a cult object (a wooden pole of some sort) associated with the worship of this deity. Such cult objects were part of a syncretistic cult in Israel which the biblical tradition clearly rejects (Dt 16:21). More than once the temple of Jerusalem was purged of its Asherah (1 Kgs 15:13; 2 Kgs 18:4; 21:7; 23:4, 6–7). The Kuntillet Ajrud inscriptions point to something beyond syncretistic cultic appurtenances. These inscriptions present Asherah as the wife of Yahweh—something the Bible never does. In the Bible, Asherah refers to an image or a cultic object; in Kuntillet Ajrud, Asherah is Yahweh's consort. Discussion of the inscription's meaning and the significance of the drawing associated with it still goes on. There are a number of issues of Hebrew grammar and comparative iconography that need to be settled before this discussion can arrive at a stage when consensus among interpreters begins to emerge.

This is the second time that archaeology has revealed the existence of Yahwists who believed that their God had a consort. The Elephantine papyri (fifth century B.C.), the last of which were published thirty years ago, provide evidence of an enclave of Yahwists in Egypt. These people too seemed to portray Yahweh with a consort. The Elephantine texts, however, refer to the "Anath of Yahu" (Yahu is a variant form of Yahweh and Anath is another Canaanite female deity). This apparent reference to a female consort of Yahweh was considered to be a local aberration. Kuntillet Ajrud shows that other Yahwists, who lived three hundred to four hundred years earlier than the group responsible for the Elephantine texts, had a similar view of Yahweh. Will Kuntillet Ajrud also be considered an aberration or will further study of the Israelite concept of God be the result? How much of the monotheism of the post-exilic period has been retrojected into texts which purport to portray beliefs of a much earlier time?

Conclusion

For the writers of classical antiquity, the Greek word *archeologia* simply meant "ancient history." In modern usage this term refers to the activities associated with the excavation, recording and interpretation of the material remains left by ancient civilizations. In its infancy, archaeology in the Middle East was dominated by a museum mentality which sought materials for display in private or public collections. Another more contemporary abuse of antiquity's material remains is to use them as pawns in the political machinations that seem to be endemic to the Middle East today. Finally because archaeology in that area has an obviously direct connection with the Bible, the relationship of the Bible and archaeology has become an issue. Obviously archaeology cannot "prove" the Bible's religious claims on those who accept it as normative for their lives. While the relationship between the Bible and archaeology is a delicate one, it ought not to be ignored. Archaeologists should not retreat into a haven that is "safe" from the problems associated with dealing with the biblical text which, of course, has survived independently of any excavations. Archaeologists, historians and exegetes need to be very careful to work out ways each can be aware of the other's concerns, methods and data. Archaeology proves nothing by itself. The material it unearths must be sifted by experts from a number of disciplines in order to gain a useful, objective and accurate portrait of antiquity.

2
The Excavation Project—
From Start to Finish

Introduction

What makes archaeology's contribution distinctive in the attempt to understand the world of antiquity is that archaeology's data come from the earth and are retrieved through the process of excavation. Excavation then is the heart of archaeology and naturally it is the focus of refinements within the discipline. The growing sophistication of archaeology is directly proportional to refinements in the process of excavation, yet excavation is only one-half of the process. A pioneer of modern archaeology once remarked: "A discovery dates only from the time of the record of it, and not from the times of its being found in the soil." The excavation project is not really finished until the results of excavation have been recorded, interpreted and reported. Any attempt to understand what is happening in biblical archaeology today needs to focus on the process of excavation from the time of the initial survey to the publication of a final report.

The Survey

In 1838 an American biblical scholar, Edward Robinson, began a series of journeys in Palestine that provided the impetus needed to begin the process of mapping this area and identifying biblical sites. Robinson's journeys and publications piqued the interest of amateurs and scholars alike in the land which was the scene of ancient Israel's history and which nourished early Judaism and Christianity alike. While Robinson was not an archaeologist himself, his work was one of the foundations upon which biblical archaeology was built. Though archaeological methods have developed steadily since the days of Robinson's travels through Palestine, surveys like the ones he pioneered are often the best way to begin an excavation project.

Unfortunately too much of the excavation in the Middle East has been "salvage" archaeology. A modern settlement is being built or enlarged, and in the course of the construction evidence of an ancient settlement is unearthed. When this happens, archaeologists are brought in to excavate quickly before all will be lost to the bulldozers. The archaeologists have little time to prepare for their operation in such circumstances. Also they have to proceed with some dispatch in these situations since the modern settlers want to get on with their projects. Arachaeology is one science that does not operate in the sterile and controlled atmosphere of a laboratory. The scene of archaeology's labors is in a living environment with modern settlements encroaching upon the archaeologist's field of labor. Salvage archaeology does not afford the optimum conditions for a well-conceived and well-controlled excavation project. Such endeavors are generally too rushed and undersupported to be completely successful, but at least the bulldozers are halted for a little while.

At the opposite extreme from the salvage operation is the massive excavation project like the one which took place over a number of years at Gezer or like the one which is still going on at Caesarea Martima. Such projects are designed to study a large site with a relatively long period of occupation. These projects usually extend over a number of years and require a great investment of funds and long-term commitment of competent personnel. While they have contributed to the development of archaeological methodology and have been the training ground for numerous archaeologists, the complexity and cost of such projects today make it quite clear that the massive excavation project is no longer feasible or even desirable. The trend today is toward smaller and more manageable projects which are carefully designed to answer specific problems.

The choice of sites for excavation is usually the result of regional surveys. These surveys recognize the impossibility of excavating every site. Difficult choices will need to be made in order to make the best use of limited resources available to the archaeologist and still shed some light on little known or neglected areas. Choosing sites for excavation requires the setting of specific goals and the establishing of a list of priorities. These tasks can be done well only after thorough surveys of particular regions. The results of the survey will sometimes determine the strategy to be employed in excavation. At times a site will be thoroughly excavated. Under a different set of circumstances excavation will be limited to a specific area within the site. The survey begins with examination of pottery sherds on the surface and study of any architectural fragments or any other evidences of ancient structures that may be visible. Occasionally the survey will involve excavating a few probe trenches to make certain that more elaborate procedures will be fruitful. The outcome of these tentative procedures will determine whether the excavation of a particular site can contribute to the solving of specific problems in a way that could justify the major investment in funds and personnel that full-scale excavation entails.

Surveys are generally made of a number of sites in a specific geographical region such as the Yoqne'am Regional Survey in the Jezreel Valley and the Meiron Excavation Project's Survey in Galilee. The object of the former survey was to determine what sites ought to be excavated in the Jezreel Valley which was replete with settlements even before the Israelite settlement. The survey of Galilee was part of a larger project whose ultimate goal is the illumination of our understanding of Galilee as a specific region with its own identity. The results of such a project would be of great importance since Galilee was a very significant locale in the development of postbiblical Judaism and early Christianity. The survey involves a systematic surface investigation and analysis of data such as size of sites and artifactual data in order to determine settlement patterns and relationships between sites. Surveys are the most economical form of field work when one considers the amount of data retrieved in relationship to the cost involved.

The Proposal

After the survey is completed, a decision needs to be made about the desirability and feasibility of launching a full-scale excavation project. Usually the results of the survey will suggest the specific objectives of the project. The next priority is to assemble a permanent staff of experts in ceramics, coins, field techniques, photography and geology among other fields. Excavation staffs today are truly interdisciplinary since the data revealed through excavation are generally too complex for a single individual to control. Additional specialists will be determined by the specific goals of the project. For example, if the site contains substantial ruins of monumental buildings, an architect is indispensable in "reconstructing" these buildings on paper once the excavation has revealed the dimensions of the buildings and after any remaining architectural fragments have been uncovered.

Archaeologists usually do not develop their projects as independent individuals. There are a number of national "schools" of archaeology in the Middle East which serve to coordinate archaeological work, provide some support services, facilitate publication and encourage professional development of and communication among archaeologists. An American school of archaeology was established in Jerusalem in 1900 and is now known as the American Schools of Oriental Research. It is made up of more than one hundred and forty member institutions (universities, colleges and seminaries) in the United States and Canada as well as twenty-five hundred individual members. ASOR has field expeditions going on in six different countries in the Middle East: Cyprus, Egypt, Israel, Jordan, Syria and Tunisia. It has research centers in Jerusalem, Israel; Amman, Jordan; and Nicosia, Cyprus. It publishes journals such as the *Biblical Archeologist,* the *Bulletin of the American Schools of Oriental Research* and the *Journal of Cuneiform Studies.*

Once the project is defined and appropriate staff members have been assembled, the next step is to make a formal request to the proper governmental agency which oversees all excavation projects undertaken within its territories. Although procedures vary from country to country, departments of antiquities exist in order to insure that only reputable persons be allowed to dig under carefully controlled circumstances. These requests for permission to dig include a description of the site to be excavated, the objectives of the project, the financial arrangements, the names of the permanent staff, and references to any previous excavation projects that may have been undertaken by the members of the staff. All this information is carefully considered by the local government in order to insure that its national archaeological treasures will be handled with the appropriate care. Unfortunately archaeologists will sometimes be caught in the tangled web of Middle Eastern politics. They may have their proposals turned down for political reasons and not for lack of scholarly credentials and archaeological experience.

A critical part of any proposal is its budgetary section. Financing an excavation project is not a simple matter. Costs have risen enormously over the years, and unless a particular project can demonstrate the financial resources to carry its work to completion, no permission can be given. One method of dealing with the problem of finances has been the rise of consortia. A number of academic institutions will band together and jointly sponsor an excavation project. These schools contribute not only by consortium payments but also through the contribution of faculty members who serve on the staff of the project. In addition these schools supply student volunteers who work in the field. Students will pay their own way to the site of the excavation and their room and board at the site as well as tuition fees, since participation in the project is often taken for academic credit. Occasionally sponsoring schools allow the expedition to finance itself out of tuition revenues.

Field Work

Once approval has been gained from the local department of antiquities and a permanent staff and sufficient volunteers have been assembled, the actual field work can begin. Obviously field work is the heart of the archaeological enterprise and is the most critical step in the process of trying to understand the world of antiquity through an analysis of its material culture. What makes archaeology different from all other disciplines which also try to understand the ancient world is that archaeology derives its data from the earth through excavation. What is so perilous about excavation is the ever-present possibility of destroying the very evidence one is trying to uncover. That is why the method employed in field work is so crucial. The dig must be carefully controlled and its progress must be meticulously recorded so that as much material as possible is uncovered and preserved for later interpretation. All the good intentions in the world will not make up for poor techniques. Once a particular area is excavated it cannot be excavated again. Archaeology is one science which cannot repeat its experiments. That is why it must be done right the first time.

American archaeologists who work in the Middle East use a particular method of excavation and recording to insure the proper control over field work. This approach to field work is called the Wheeler-Kenyon method since its basic methodology is taken from Mortimer Wheeler's *Archaeology from the Earth* and Kathleen Kenyon's *Beginning in Archaeology*. While there may be differences in the application of specific strategies of this method among individual archaeologists, there is general agreement on the principles of excavation which are the heart of the Wheeler-Kenyon method.

The goal of this method of excavation is to enable anyone to reconstruct a three-dimensional model of an excavation site on the basis of the recorded data. To achieve this end, excavation must be stratigraphic, i.e., the archaeologist must peel off one soil layer (stratum) at a time and carefully record the composition and contents of that layer. The goal of stratigraphic excavation is to transform archaeology from being destructive and intrusive treasure-hunting into a systematic and scientific discipline whose purpose is to illuminate the cultural process and reconstruct human behavior on the basis of material remains.

Field work begins with clearing the site of all vegetation in order to get a clear picture of the area to be excavated and any structures or architectural fragments that may be above ground. Once this is completed, it is possible to survey the area and lay out N-S and E-W grids that will serve as reference points for the placement of the squares which will be excavated. Once the survey of the site is complete and the grids laid, a decision is made with regard to placing the squares since the entire site is usually not excavated. Placing of the squares is determined by the goals of the project and the available personnel. For example, if the major goal of a project is to excavate a monumental building such as a synagogue, most of the work would need to be directed at clarifying the building's history and its relationship to the surrounding area and structures.

Before excavation can begin, a very practical decision needs to be made: where to locate the sifter and the dump. In most projects the use of a sifter is necessary, especially when the site can be expected to yield small artifacts such as coins, nails, jewelry and other small objects that can be missed by the most careful excavator. Before any soil is discarded, it needs to be sifted to avoid throwing away important material with the soil accumulated over the centuries. Sifting takes place near the dump. This dump must be placed away from any area which may be excavated at some later date but not too far away from the excavation so that valuable time is taken up by trips to a distant dump.

Work can now proceed on the square to be excavated. Usually the area to be excavated is a five-meter square. Another meter on each side is set aside for balks, which are unexcavated strips left standing between areas. The actual size and shape of each "square" can vary according to the nature of the site being excavated but it must be large enough to allow an efficient use of personnel and small enough to maintain adequate control over the digging. Each square is marked off with string anchored to metal stakes, one of which becomes a datum point whose elevation is used in determining the elevation of the square as work proceeds on it. The taking of elevations throughout the process of excavation is important in order to preserve a three-dimensional record of the excavation.

The digging begins with the sinking of a small probe trench at one end of the square. Excavation in the probe trench proceeds rather quickly. The purpose of the probe is to reveal the stratification (layering) of the square. The probe then becomes a guide to the excavators as they remove the successive layers encountered in the square. Once the probe has clarified the stratigraphy of the area, the rest of the square can be excavated more carefully and intelligently. To maintain control and to avoid too much destruction, digging is done with hand tools: trowels and small hand picks. It is important that the excavator dig "cleanly"; loose dirt must be removed so that excavators can see what they are doing. In addition, throughout the excavation of the probe and the rest of the square careful attention needs to be paid to the balks. They provide a visible record of the various strata of the square. Such a record is important in trying to clarify the stratigraphy of the individual areas and of the site as a whole. Balks are indispensable tools in analyzing the sequence of layers as well as in maintaining strict control over excavation.

The goal of stratigraphic excavation is to expose the occupational phases of the site one at a time. The probe helps to define these phases and to guide their removal. When a probe is completed, it becomes possible to expose all the features (artifacts, walls, architectural fragments) of a given layer with proper control. Occasionally one comes across instrusive elements such as pits, fills and burials. These need to be excavated separately since they are not associated with the original use of the site but were introduced at a later date. Once the occupational layer and associated features are revealed, they are carefully cleaned and photographed before another probe is sunk to prepare for the excavation of the next phase. This procedure continues until every occupational layer of the site has been exposed. The excavators know that their work is completed once they come to bedrock or virgin soil. Without the careful and disciplined layer-by-layer excavation, it is impossible to determine the sequence of a site's occupational history.

Recording

The results of the most meticulously done stratigraphic excavation will be lost unless the progress of the digging is recorded. The more careful and complete the recording system employed, the more certain will be the synthesis of the data uncovered thorugh excavation. An important component of any recording system is the field notes of the archaeologist. Field notes of the early archaeologists were little more than diaries. Today, however, a systematic approach to field notes is an integral feature of the Wheeler-Kenyon method of archaeology. A step-by-step record of excavation makes possible the reconstruction of the actual progress of the dig months and even years later. In addition to the factual data recorded, field notes are also used by the archaeologists to record tentative interpretations and hypotheses made on the spot while the excavation is in progress. Proposing and testing hypotheses in the course of excavation is an important part of maintaining control over the excavation.

In addition to the field notes there are other components of a

Khirbet Shema', Locus Sheet for Walls
IDENTIFICATION: Locus _3029____
  Largest wall in square, to north
  Dimensions   Recording
1. Preserved length _5.00 m_   33. Date of best sketch _6/27/72_
2. Preserved width _55-62 cm._   Date of architect's drawing _6/29/72_
3. Preserved max. height _1.03 m_   34. Photos:_____
4. Top elevations _749.23 to 749.04 (W-E)_ _____
5. Founding elevs. _748.03 to 748.00 (W-E)_ Stratigraphic Relationships
                                      6. Foundation trench No. _3047_
  Construction
15. Rows wide _2_   7. Founded on bedrock? _no_
16. Rubble core? _no_   8. Bonds with wall(s): _none_
17. Courses high _4 max._   9. Butts with wall(s): _3033 onto 3029_
18. Av. Size of stones _50X30X25_   10. Associated loci: _floor 3036, 3038, 3039_
19. Field stones _foundation only_   11. Associated features _door at E. end_
20. Hammer dressed _yes_   12. Disturbed by: _modern robbing_
21. Drafted margins, with boss_____ 13. Cuts into: _3045, 3046_
22. Drafted margins, cut face _3 stones_ 14. Identical locus in adjoining areas
23. Keyed for plaster _S. face_   _2926 , 3107_
24. No. courses in foundation _2_   Location
                                      30. Where in square? _north end_
25. No. finished faces _none_   In which balk? _W, E_
26. No. plastered faces _South face_ 31. Direction it runs _W → E_
27. Mortared? _no_   32. Evident function _N wall of_
28. Repaired or Rebuilt? _yes_   _house also in NE 29, NE 31,_
29. where _west end, 3 stones (see 22.)_ _NE 23, NE 24, NE 25_

Mention dates _6/19/72; 6/20; 6/21/72; 6/22/72; 6/27; 6/29; 6/30_

Additional data_____

Bucket No.   Date   Reading   Artifacts
none
_____
_____

21

good recording system. The first of these is the top plan which is a diagram of the area being excavated as viewed from above. Such a plan is drawn to scale on graph paper for each day of excavation. The top plan shows all the exposed features of the area under excavation: walls, floors, stairs, column bases. It also is used to locate the exact spot and elevation where particular artifacts were found in the course of digging. Elevations of the square at the beginning and end of the day are noted on the top plan so that the progress of each day's work is clear.

The top plan is interpreted through the field notes which are a verbal description of each day's work. In these notes, anything of archaeological significance is recorded. It is not intended to be a finished product, but is simply a journal where the raw data are recorded. Synthesis of the data comes later once the project is completed. Field notes help make this synthesis both possible and reliable since whatever is not recorded will be forgotten. The value of the final report of the entire project is directly proportional to the quality of the field notes taken in the course of the digging. Very often the area supervisors need to devote most of their time in the field to the notebook; the actual excavation is left to others.

A third component of the recording system is the locus sheet. A locus (plural: loci) is the smallest unit of stratigraphy. Each stratum is made up of many loci. A locus may be a wall, a floor, a drain, an oven, earth or debris. For recording purposes each locus is assigned a different number. The locus sheets, which are arranged numerically, contain all the information necessary to provide a thorough description of the locus. Besides information such as the make-up, color, size and contents of each locus, its relationship to surrounding loci is noted. Most projects have standardized forms for noting all this information. Precise description of each locus is vital since eventually most loci will be removed in order to proceed with the excavation of the next stratum. Archaeology is the one science that systematically destroys its own evidence. That is why recording is so crucial.

Photography is clearly one of the best aids to accurate recording. Sometimes excavators will use polaroid-type photographs and include them as part of the field notes. Such photos provide another means of illustrating the comments and descriptions made in the field notes. More important are the final record photographs. These

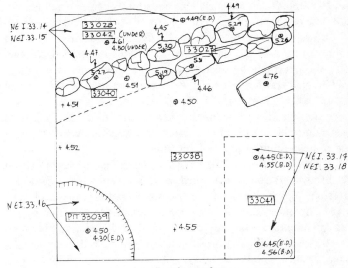

Sample top plan

are important aids to those responsible for publishing final reports. Record photos are taken of imporant loci that make up a particular phase of the site's occupation. Sometimes these photos will be published as part of the final report in order to illustrate significant parts of the report. Recently photography and computer technology have been linked into a system called photogrammetric recording. This system makes possible a three-dimensional analysis of data—something not possible in ordinary photography. Photogrammetric recording is certainly a major advance in the techniques of recording, analyzing and comparing data. In effect, this system permits the taking of "stereo" photographs. A good photographic record is helpful in another important way—it aids in public relations and fund-raising. Interesting pictures of the progress made by a project go a long way in convincing supporters that the project is worthy of continued financial aid.

Balk drawings make up the final visual record of the stratigraphy of each area under excavation. These drawings are made to scale with every feature of the balk included—every last stone. Lines are drawn in to indicate the exact places where the separation between strata are visible. Each locus is identified and its composition is indicated by use of a series of conventional signs. A well-done balk drawing is an important help to the archaeologist who must read and interpret the field notes. Balk drawings are also a needed complement to the photographic record which preserves only two dimensions. The balk dawing is an accurate representation of the vertical dimension which is of critical importance to stratigraphic excavation. Finally drawing balks in the field forces the archaeologist to make stratigraphic sense out of excavation while it is still in progress instead of postponing it until a later time.

The last component of the recording system is a series of lists on which all artifacts found are noted. Separate lists will be made for coins, stone objects, architectural fragments, pottery, metal objects, glass and any other kind of object which was made and used by the ancient inhabitants of the site. Each object is assigned a number, and the precise location where it was found is noted as well as its identification and date if known. All these data are necessary to insure that an informed judgment can be made about the relationship of each artifact to the context in which it was found. Without such judgments, the artifacts are little more than relics. Of course, the evidence gleaned from an analysis of the artifactual data can tell quite a bit about the occupational history of the site as well as provide an economic, religious and cultural profile of its ancient inhabitants.

The process of excavation is arranged in such a way as to facilitate uniform and orderly record-keeping. Without accurate recording of data, the archaeological enterprise ceases to be a scientific discipline. Good field notes provide a good data base for analysis and interpretation. These data are included in the final report so that those examining the report have an idea of the progress of the excavation and can check the interpretations made by the excavators. Without the availability of these records, the final report of the excavation project will have to be accepted "on faith." The value of such reports is obviously quite limited.

Analysis and Interpretation

While the basic work of every excavation takes place at the site being dug, very important work goes on in the camp after the day's work in the field is completed and in the laboratory after the archaeologists have returned home. The artifacts uncovered in the course of excavation must be analyzed. One goal of this analysis is to reconstruct the chronology of the site. In other words, it is necessary to date the various strata that appear in the course of the excavation in order to determine when and for how long the site was occupied. Besides developing a chronology of the site, analysis of the artifacts helps illuminate the cultural dynamics of the site. This is vital in developing a profile of the site's inhabitants. Were they wealthy or poor? Farmers, craftsmen or tradesmen? What were the economic, political and religious relationships with surrounding areas? What was their aesthetic sense? Their religious leanings? Why did the occupation cease? Did the inhabitants leave freely or were they driven out? Were they driven out by disease, famine, earthquakes, drought or perhaps by some enemy? These are the kinds of questions that sensitive and inquisitive archaeologists ask as they examine the pottery, coins, jewelry, glass, ash, and the other remnants of an ancient settlement.

Pottery

The most common artifact found is pottery. It is simply everywhere. At first, neophyte archaeologists are captivated by the knowledge that the sherds which they have recovered are more than one thousand years old, but the novelty soon wears off because of the great quantities of ceramic materials which need to be recovered, washed and read. What makes pottery so important to the archaeologist is its usefulness in dating the stratum in which it was found. Though pottery is relatively fragile, it does not decay. Pottery that was discarded in antiquity is still available for discovery by the modern excavator. Another quality of pottery which makes it particularly helpful in dating is that most forms were rather inexpensive and therefore readily discarded when broken or no longer useful. This makes it possible to assume that the pottery found in a particular stratum was manufactured and used not very long before the end of that stratum. One caution that needs to be taken due to the sheer quantity of pottery available is the vigilance so that control is exercised in the collection of the pottery from a particular locus. At the end of each day's work, the pottery collected that day is washed so that its color, ware and composition are readable by those specially skilled in the identification of ceramic material.

Reading and classification of pottery is possible because pottery like any other product of human culture demonstrates both order and variation. Pottery was used by the ancients for a number of different purposes: the storage of liquids and solids, cooking, and as tableware. Pottery used for each purpose took on certain predictable forms. Over the years these forms changed for both practical and aesthetic reasons, but these changes usually took place gradually. It did not take long for archaeologists to observe that these changes can be very helpful in dating. Consider the ceramic lamp. Over the years the technology of lighting a room did not change very much: a little oil was placed in a lamp and a burning wick which floated in the oil provided the illumination. The shape of the lamps, however, did change perceptibly over the centuries. These changes improved the efficiency of the lamps somewhat, but mostly they were the result of a desire to introduce more decorative motifs in lamp design. The ceramic lamp changed over the years from being purely functional to being a quite ornate and beautiful object. Similar developments took place in the form of other ceramic objects.

One measure of the distinctive character of a period's technological achievements, material prosperity and artistic sense was its pottery. Salient features of ceramic forms make the development of a relative chronology rather simple. To the experienced eye, an individual piece of pottery will reveal quite a bit of information: its size, its function, its ware (the appearance of the fired clay), the technique of its manufacture and even the origin of the clay out of which it was made. Certainly a basic skill for any accomplished archaeologist is the ability to recognize pottery types and to date ceramic forms. The value of pottery is not limited to establishing a chronology for the site. The ratio of imported to domestic types, fine to crude wares, and domestic to commercial forms helps to create a profile of the people who used these materials. Pottery reveals something about culture as well as about chronology.

Coins

There is quite a friendly rivalry between ceramicists and numismatists regarding the relative value of pottery and coins in determining the archaeological periods being excavated. The great advantage coins have is that they can be given an absolute date with confidence. The inscriptions on coins usually make it quite clear when they were minted. The chief disadvantage with coins is that their intrinsic value keeps them in use as a medium of exchange for a period of time after they were first minted. In other words, when a coin is found in a particular locus, the excavator can conclude that the latest occupation of the locus could not have been before the coin was minted. More precise dating for the locus can be determined only by reading pottery and other artifacts. Pottery whose forms underwent the kinds of typological developments described above can provide the archaeologist with more precise dating for the occupation of the stratum though making these dates absolute is not always possible. In any case, the coins and pottery found in a given stratum provide quite enough information to allow the archaeologist to make relatively secure conclusions in dating that stratum.

Coins were introduced into the Middle East during the Persian period (sixth to fourth century B.C.) and by the Hellenistic (fourth to first century B.C.) and Roman (first century B.C. to fourth century A.D.) periods they were in wide usage. Coins were made out of three different materials: gold, silver and bronze. Since the bronze coins had the least intrinsic value, one can assume that they were in the widest currency and were not as carefully hoarded as were the more valuable silver and gold. Similarly it is unlikely that bronze coins were melted down in order to reuse their metal as much as was the case of the silver and gold coins; as a result, there are far more bronze coins available for discovery by the sharp-eyed excavator. Unfortunately bronze coins corrode quite badly and usually require careful cleaning before they are readable. Occasionally a bronze coin will be so corroded as to make any reading impossible. Silver and especially gold coins withstand the elements much better and are more easily cleaned and prepared for reading. Most excavators who work on sites with significant levels from the Roman period and later will have a numismatist on staff who can make identification of coins in the field in order that the information gleaned from the coins can help with the formulation of preliminary hypotheses and occasionally help to direct digging strategy.

As in the case with pottery, coins can tell the archaeologist more than the date of a site's occupation. The location of the mint where the coins were found at a particular site can give some indication of that site's economic ties. The number and kind of coins found may give a clue to the relative prosperity of the site's inhabitants. Some coins are inscribed with illustrations of important buildings which were destroyed in antiquity, and thus they preserve the depiction of the building which would otherwise be unknown. Coins sometimes picture the important agricultural products of a particular region. Finally coins were often used as tools of religious and political propaganda, and therefore they give some hints of the sympathies of the ancients who inhabited the site. Coins provide an invaluable look into the culture of antiquity.

Other Evidence

Besides coins and pottery, excavation uncovers many other artifacts such as glass objects, metal objects (nails, hinges, tools), architectural fragments (columns, bases, and capitals), stone implements (wine and olive presses) and jewelry among other things. All these are carefully excavated, recorded, cleaned, catalogued and, if possible, restored. Analysis of such objects helps archaeologists develop a more complete picture of the site and its inhabitants. For example, when the excavation of large public buildings reveals architectural fragments with intricate decorative motifs, this may indicate a community which was more wealthy than one whose public buildings were rather simple and austere. All artifactual evidence needs to be preserved and interpreted so that we can recognize the people who made and used them centuries ago. Finally, it is becoming very clear that archaeologists cannot limit their attention to manufactured objects if they want to draw a complete picture of conditions in antiquity. Soil analysis can reveal much about the climatic conditions.

Examination of seeds can show that plants grew in either a wild or domesticated state. Study of human bones can help identify the diet and health of the ancients. Analysis of animal bones can reveal something about their economy and agricultural practices. The archaeologist today looks for any scrap of evidence that the ground will give up in order to better understand and describe the ancient world.

Restoration

One final aspect of field work that needs to be mentioned is restoration. Archaeologists have always tried to restore artifacts to their original state when feasible. Sometimes enough pieces of a broken ceramic object will be found that a skilled technician can put the object back together as if it were a three-dimensional jigsaw puzzle. Restoring pottery not only preserves a record of the excavation's achievements but provides examples of complete pottery types for study. When it is possible to restore glass objects, a dig will have preserved some of the more beautiful artifacts that are found in the course of excavation. In recent years these restoration efforts were extended beyond small artifacts to large structures. Some archaeologists not only excavate a site but try to reuse the architectural fragments remaining on the site in an effort to reconstruct the ancient buildings to some extent. Governments encourage such efforts and sometimes even augment them with the hope of preserving their archaeological heritage. Important sites like Qumran, Megiddo and Masada have been excavated, restored and turned into national parks in which the non-professional can get a good introduction to archaeology by simply walking through the site.

Reports

With the completion of work in the field, the work of excavators is just beginning since archaeologists who are ready to dig must be willing to publish the results of their excavations. This is the only way that individual archaeologists can share findings with one another. While the dig itself may be exciting and immediately rewarding, publication is often experienced as tedious, frustrating and too costly. For these and other reasons, the pace of final publications has not always kept up with the pace of excavation. This, of course, is a very regrettable situation.

In general most archaeologists working in the field publish some type of report of onging activity in periodicals like the *Israel Exploration Journal* and *Revue Biblique* which set aside space for just such a purpose. These reports are quite brief and generally summarize the results of field work. They tend to highlight unusual finds and sometimes even advance a tentative interpretation of data. Their purpose is to keep an interested audience apprised of current projects. A more complete report of a preliminary nature is sometimes published in which more technical summaries are provided. Usually these reports will be illustrated with photographs of important strata and of significant artifactual finds. They may also include to-scale drawings of pottery types and architectural plans. These preliminary reports are usually published in professional archaeological journals such as the *Bulletin of the American Schools of Oriental Research*. Attempts at synthesizing the data are kept to a minimum or are put off entirely until the final report.

While most archaeologists will publish brief reports on the progress of the excavation projects and some publish excellent preliminary reports, too few have published final reports. In fact, some archaeologists have died without publishing final reports on their major excavations. The most embarrassing admission that archaeologists have to make is that the bulk of excavated material remains unpublished.

When a final report is made, archaeologists have to be descriptive to a great extent. They need to report their findings in such a way that all the archaeological evidence they used in arriving at their analysis and conclusions about a particular site is presented to the reader. No conclusion found in the final report should be accepted on faith. One of the principal features of the final report will be its illustrations: photographs, balk drawings, architect's drawings, drawings of pottery types. The report also contains the lists of artifacts found plus their identification. Finally the report describes all the various types of laboratory analyses considered necessary to provide as complete a profile of the ancient site as modern technology permits.

The value of a final report is diminished if it is confined to description alone. There needs to be a synthesis of the vast amount of data unearthed over seasons of excavation. While archaeologists are in general agreement regarding the need for control in excavation and employ recognized methods to insure that control, there is no consensus on the conrols needed in the interpretation. Some are carefully formulated and therefore highly probable, occasionally some are quite controversial, and a few are even fanciful. One concern of archaeologists today is to find a theoretical model that can provide a framework within which to make an objective synthesis. The Wheeler-Kenyon method has supplied control in excavation; there needs to be some model to provide control in synthesis and interpretation.

An important aspect of the synthesis of data is the correlation of this data to the literature of antiquity if possible. This task is full of dangers because there is the temptation to make quick and easy comparisons. Sometimes an ancient text such as the Bible will guide the interpretation of the archaeological data. The data then becomes support for a certain interpretation of the text in question. There is the constant danger of circular reasoning in this situation. Another problem is the bias that certain ancient texts have. This bias can show up in the interpretation of excavated material. Again it is clear that there is a need for a general theory to help understand the phenomena revealed in the course of excavation.

The Future of Field Work

The successful completion of an excavation project from the initial survey to the publication of a final report is the result of a substantial investment of time, talent and money. Even a small project with rather limited objectives requires a serious commitment from its permanent staff and financial supporters in order that the project can achieve its goals and issue a report that will be a genuine contribution to our knowledge of antiquity. The days of the vast projects are numbered not only because of the difficulty in keeping the project solvent but also because of the complexity of the data uncovered by modern archaeological techniques. It is clear that one person cannot keep adequate control over these data. There is just too much. In view of this increasing sophistication of archaeological methodology, projects are being scaled down to more manageable levels and are being administered by a group of archaeologists acting as a team. The team approach to more modestly conceived projects appears to be a more efficient way to operate in the field. Even though the survey is the most cost efficient method, at times full-scale excavation will be necessary, but the by-word of excavation is "to get more from less." Archaeologists need to plan their projects in such a way that clearly stated objectives can be met with a reasonable investment of time and money and so that results can be effectively communicated to the scholarly community.

At times, however, it does seem as though field archaeologists are caught in a "Catch-22" situation. The growing sophistication of the techniques of archaeology often requires an investment in more costly equipment. In other words, it costs more money just to keep abreast with the latest methods. For example, the use of computer technology for the storage, retrieval, correlation and interpretation of information will very soon become standard practice for all projects. The usefulness of computer technology is limited only by the imagination of those who employ it. Using this new tool will require not only a financial outlay from the limited resources of archaeological projects but also the professional development of archaeologists who need to learn the potential of this new tool. The computer is one of the ways that archaeologists can "get more from less."

Volunteers

Even with a competent staff, adequate financial support and the latest technology, the success of nearly every excavation project is dependent upon volunteer help. Volunteers pay their own way and give their time to do the basic work of excavation projects—moving dirt. If projects had to hire people to do the type of work done by volunteers, their budgets would swell to prohibitive size. Usually volunteers are students for whom field archaeology is part of their academic program, but there is a significant number of people whose sole motivation is an unquenchable fascination with the world of antiquity—a fascination that finds field archaeology the ultimate experience. It is one thing to read accounts of excavation projects; it is quite another to have first-hand experience on a dig. It is one thing to read history books; it is quite another to help write them. Most projects solicit volunteer help. A popular periodical, the *Biblical Archaeology Review*, usually lists the projects which welcome volunteers. There is no better way for someone with an interest in archaeology to pursue that interest than to volunteer for a dig. While this will involve no small personal investment, most volunteers consider the experience well worth the time, money and perspiration it entails. While volunteers make an invaluable contribution to any excavation project, the project itself makes possible an unique experience in the life of each volunteer.

The keys to success for any excavation project are many: good planning by a skilled staff, excavation and recording techniques that facilitate adequate control over the data, the use of the latest technology in the synthesis of the data, solid financial support, a commitment to publication and a good number of generous volunteers. It is a complex formula, but an excavation project is a complex undertaking.

3
Ebla—Controversy and Promise

Located some fifty-five kilometers from Aleppo in northwest Syria, Tell Mardikh has been the site of an archaeological project sponsored by the Italian Archaeological Mission in Syria since 1964. A *tell* is an artificial mound created by heaping up successive layers of human occupation over a very long period of time. Tell Mardikh is a relatively large site comprising fifty-six hectares (about one hundred and thirty-eight acres). When an excavation project begins archaeologists have some expectations about what they expect to find, but the spectacular results from the Mardikh project were beyond everyone's expectations. Unfortunately the story of the project is not an entirely happy one. While Tell Mardikh has the promise of adding significantly to our knowledge of the ancient Near East, up until now the project has been the center of a serious international scholarly and political controversy.

Like any other human endeavor, archaeology is subject to the vagaries of its all too human practitioners. What is supposedly a scientific discipline can degenerate into a battlefield where personal, professional, religious and even political wars are waged. Tell Mardikh is a case in point. Since its inception the project has been directed by Paolo Matthiae, an archaeologist and art historian. In 1969, Giovanni Pettinato, a Sumerologist (an expert in the language of ancient Sumer), was called in to decipher an inscription on a statue found in the course of that year's excavation. On the basis of his translation of that inscription, Pettinato suggested that Tell Mardikh was ancient Ebla, a city known from ancient sources but whose location was in doubt. Pettinato's work convinced Matthiae that Mardikh was Ebla, though not all scholars agreed at first. Analysis of additional texts uncovered at Mardikh over the years has confirmed Pettinato's initial identification. The collaboration between Matthiae and Pettinato should have been a harbinger of future cooperation. Unfortunately it was not.

The Controversy

Pettinato became formally associated with Matthiae's project at Ebla in 1974 when some forty inscribed clay tablets were found. Matthiae himself could not read the cuneiform (wedge-shaped script) in which these ancient texts were written so he turned again to Pettinato for help. The next year's excavations unearthed the royal archives of Ebla with its rich store of tablets. Over the next few years more tablets were found until some seventeen thousand tablets came to light. Both Matthiae and Pettinato knew that they had made an extraordinary find—the kind that archaeologists dream about. Unfortunately the seventeen thousand tablets simply set the stage for a dramatic falling out between Matthiae and Pettinato. Their disagreements began with the dates each set for the tablets. On the basis of stratigraphy and ceramic typology, Matthiae dated the tablets to 2400–2200 B.C. On the basis of epigraphy (the style of writing), Pettinato dated them to 2580–2450 B.C. Pettinato's dating meant that Matthiae's stratigraphy was incorrect and that he may have missed an entire stratum in the course of his excavations. Since neither the archaeologist nor the epigrapher was willing to retreat from his position, matters could get only worse—and they did.

The problems between Matthiae and Pettinato were compounded by the inevitable media-hype which usually follows any kind of an important discovery such as the royal archives of Ebla with its thousands of tablets. The interest of the media in the United States resulted from the so-called parallels and connections that supposedly existed between the Bible and the tablets from Ebla. These connections were touted by a prominent and respected American biblical scholar, David Noel Freedman. He took it upon himself to visit the two Italians and was so impressed with the information about Ebla which they shared with him that he arranged an American lecture tour for them. The highlight of this tour was Pettinato's address to the annual meeting of the Society of Biblical Literature at St. Louis in 1976. In that address Pettinato announced to his fellow scholars that he found the names of the five cities of the plain (Sodom, Gomorrah, Admah, Zeboiim and Bela; cf. Gen 14) on a single tablet from Ebla listed in the very same order as in the Bible. That was all that an admitted conservative scholar like Freedman needed in order to reassert his convictions about this historicity of the traditions in the Book of Genesis. Recent literary studies of the patriarchal narratives (Gen 12—50) have suggested that these traditions tell us nothing about any presumed patriarchal era since they are creations of later periods in ancient Israel's history. Freedman has characterized these views as examples of skepticism and sophistry now undercut by the tablets from Ebla. Freedman believed that Ebla had finally provided the kind of rigorous scientific data that he had always sought.

Freedman was joined in his campaign to promote the connections between the Bible and the tablets from Ebla by the prolific Jesuit expert on Semitic languages, Mitchell Dahood. Like Freedman, Dahood was convinced that the Ebla tablets demonstrated that Genesis contains truly historical traditions which date from a period long before ancient Israel achieved its national identity. Dahood remarked that it was ironic that archaeologists were uncovering and deciphering the Ebla tablets about the same time literary analysis of Genesis was questioning the historicity of the patriarchal narratives. Dahood also believed that the study of the Ebla tablets would help clarify puzzling passages in the Hebrew Bible. His lectures and writings came to be replete with references to how Ebla has improved our ability to understand biblical Hebrew (see his "Are the Ebla Tablets Relevant to Biblical Research?" *Biblical Archaeology Review* 6 [1980] 54–60). Not all of Dahood's colleagues have accepted all of his conclusions, though they admired the creativity he displayed in formulating his provocative suggestions.

Certainly the most controversial of all Pettinato's suggestions has been his contention that a god named Ya or Yaw was part of the pantheon in Ebla. Even though Dahood was quick to lend his support to Pettinato, not all Semiticists agreed with Pettinato's reading of the tablets supposedly containing evidence of a god Ya(w) worshiped at Ebla. There is no direct evidence of the presence of Ya(w) among the gods of Ebla, since this name does not appear on any lists of the divinities associated with Ebla though such lists have been found and deciphered. Pettinato's evidence is indirect. Among the various economic documents which he has translated, Pettinato believes that he has come across names with a theophorous element which he reads as Ya. Theophorous names in which a name of a god becomes part of an individual's personal name are common enough throughout the ancient Near East so that Pettinato's suggestion is plausible. Among the theophorous names from Ebla, Pettinato includes Mi-ka-ya (Who is like Ya?), Ish-ma-ya (Ya has heard), and En-na-ya (Have pity, O Ya). Some Semiticists consider Pettinato's readings somewhat premature because not enough is known about how Ebla's scribes modified the cuneiform system of writing the Sumerian language to their own "Eblaite" language. In other words, it may be that the symbol which Pettinato reads as Ya may actually be representing an entirely different word since cuneiform symbols can have multiple meanings. Determination of the exact meaning of a particular symbol is dependent upon the context in which the symbol is found and local methods of using cuneiform writing. Many scholars believe that not enough is known about the language to make a definitive judgment about the Ya-names.

Pettinato's observations about the Ya-names went a bit further than simply positing their existence. He claimed that tablets from the reign of Ebrum, one of Ebla's kings, show a substitution of Ya-names for Il-names. Il is another theophorous element. In other words, before Ebrum was king a popular name would have been Mi-ka-il (Who is like Il?). With Ebrum's accession the name would have changed to Mi-ka-ya. This observation led Pettinato to speak of a "religious revolution" supposedly occurring during the reign of Ebrum when Il was supplanted by Ya. This suggestion has been questioned by a number of leading scholars, with the exception of Dahood who remained convinced of Pettinato's readings until his untimely death in 1982. The safest conclusion that can be drawn from the scholarly controversies which have swirled around Pettinato's readings is that much more study of the tablets from Ebla is required before it will be possible to reach a consensus as to how they are to be read. The fact that cuneiform signs have more than one possible reading complicates the process. Only after careful collabo-

rative work by a number of scholars will these tablets be read with
some measure of confidence.

At one point Pettinato had to admit that some of his preliminary readings were premature. After all of the excitement regarding
his assertions about the five cities of the plain in the biblical sequence
on a tablet from Ebla, Pettinato conceded that there was no tablet on
which all the five cities were named. When asked about this reversal
of position, Pettinato denied that this amounted to a retraction, because he had made the suggestion about the cities of the plain in a
speech rather than in writing, and one can retract only what one has
written. Pettinato should have remembered that the speech was giv-
en to thousands of American biblical scholars who were ready to believe what they heard from a colleague regarding his reading of
important tablets which were under his sole control.

The controversy regarding the cities of the plain and the Ya-
names point to the need for more rapid publication of ancient texts.
Formal publication of such texts usually includes a readable photograph of the text, a hand-drawn copy of the text which makes it easier to read than the photograph, a complete transliteration of the text,
a translation and a short commentary. By this standard only a small
fraction of Ebla tablets have been published, though Pettinato and
his supporters have made many references to their contents. In the
meantime, scholars must rely on those who have these texts in their
possession for more accurate accounts of their contents than Pettinato gave in his speech before the Society of Biblical Literature in
1976. Unless he was ready to publish the texts which supported his
statements, Pettinato should not have made statements which he
knew would cause wonderment among his fellow scholars. Without
published texts, there was no way that his colleagues could make an
independent assessment of his readings.

It was not long before Pettinato's assertions were popularized
through accounts on the wire services and in magazines like *News-
week* (November 15, 1976), *National Geographic* (December, 1978,
pp. 730–759) and the *Biblical Archaeology Review,* which published a
whole spate of articles on Ebla. These accounts fueled popular imagination especially among conservative and fundamentalist Christians
who saw Ebla as supporting the historicity of the Bible. These people
were ready to identify Pettinato's Ya(w) with the Yahweh of ancient

Israel and his Ebrum with Eber, one of Abraham's ancestors (Gen 11:14). To his credit Pettinato himself did not make these connections, but he would have to be incredibly naive not to think that they would be made. That is all the more reason for strict adherence to a policy of rapid publication of important texts, especially when there is a danger that such data might be misunderstood and misused.

Besides the connections with Genesis 14 and with the name Yahweh, Pettinato and his supporters have indicated that the tablets contain a creation and flood story similar to those in Genesis. We are told that the tablets mention the names of cities which play an important role in the Bible: Hazor, Megiddo, Gaza, Salem, Joppa and Jerusalem among others. They also tell us that Ebla will provide a definitive location for Abraham's birthplace, the city of Ur. Personal names such as Abram, Esau, Israel, Michael, Saul and David supposedly appear in the tablets. Finally Pettinato claims that, like ancient Israel, Ebla had judges, prophets and kings and that Ebla anointed her kings. This is quite a potpourri of biblical connections. When pressed for the hard evidence for these assertions, Pettinato has retreated for the most part. In the words of one commentator on this perplexing state of affairs, the evidence of biblical connections seemed "to evaporate."

While all this was being played out in scholarly and popular circles, the Syrian authorities in whose country Tell Mardikh is located were becoming disturbed by all these references to connections between the third millennium site to a late second to first century phenomenon which we call ancient Israel. Why was there such a rush to connect these two when they were separated by more than one thousand years in antiquity? This great discovery relating to their own cultural heritage was being valued not on its own merits but in terms of what it reveals about ancient Israel. Secondly, since ancient religious traditions have been used to support the territorial claims of modern political states in the Middle East, it was quite understandable that the Syrians were afraid that a few Ebla tablets would be thrown onto the negotiating table. In any case, the Syrian government requested and received a declaration by Pettinato which repudiated what he called the "pretended links" of Ebla with the Bible. This action led to accusations that the Syrians were trying to influence the study of Ebla in order to play down connections with the

Bible (see *Biblical Archaeology Review* 5 [1979] 37–50). Such provocative statements cannot obscure the reality: Pettinato's premature
readings of some tablets which were naively accepted by some scholars were really responsible for all the controversy.

All this did nothing but exacerbate the deteriorating relationship that existed between Matthiae and Pettinato. As head of the excavation project, Matthiae thought it was his responsibility to
oversee the publication of the Ebla tablets, so he appointed a ten-
member commission to coordinate translation and publication. As
the epigrapher of the Mardikh project, Pettinato thought that he
should have been in charge of the publication of the tablets. The tensions between the two grew until Pettinato broke off all connections
with Matthiae who replaced him as epigrapher with Alfonso Archi
who set about refuting most of Pettinato's work. This ridiculous situation has degenerated even more with the insults and accusations
that the parties to this dispute hurl at one another. It has spawned
rival journals, books and international symposia. Ebla has become an
object lesson on how not to handle an archaeological project.

Promise

The only way one can objectively assess the value of the spectacular finds at Ebla is to ignore the polemics and journalistic jargon
that have been unwelcome components of the way information about
Ebla has been disseminated among scholars and the general public
alike. Too much has been made of the tenuous and meager material
that has been released so far. Before the publication of more texts, it
makes little sense to assume definitive positions that will probably
have to be re-examined more than once. Calm, careful and unbiased
study of all available material is the first priority of scholarship. Actually this has all happened before but apparently we have not
learned from the past. The discoveries at Ugarit, Mari and Nuzi in
the 1930's and at Qumran in the 1950's were proclaimed as "revolutionary" with regard to the impact they would have on biblical studies. Over the years data from these sites have been studied,
assimilated and applied to a previously existing body of knowledge.
The result has been greater understanding, refinement of concepts,
growth in scholarship—but no revolution. The same will be true of

Tell Mardikh from the south-east

Ebla. Once the calm of dispassionate scholarship takes over the study of the Ebla tablets, their undoubted value will be impressive indeed.

Even if no tablets were ever found at Ebla, the other archaeological finds themselves would be of great importance because they reveal information about Syria in the third millennium B.C. that was previously unknown. The excavations at Mardikh have uncovered an advanced urban civilization with impressive monumental architecture and a developed esthetic sense that few believed existed. The Semitic people who created this advanced culture in the middle of the third millennium must have arrived in the region centuries earlier, but this contradicts previous historical reconstructions which viewed Syria as a cultural backwater at this time. The great centers of civili-

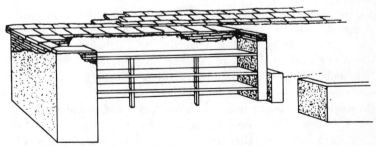

Wall Shelves for tablets in the Archive room of the Ebla Palace G.

zation were Egypt to the southwest and Mesopotamia to the south-east. The population of Syria was supposedly composed of nomadic shepherds or semi-nomadic pastoralists who had a very primitive level of material culture. The discovery of ancient Ebla makes it impossible to describe the territory between Egypt and Mesopotamia as a cultural wasteland populated by illiterate barbarians. Ebla of the third millennium was a major urban center with an advanced and sophisticated material culture.

The level of Ebla's culture has been indicated by the remains of its buildings and other artifacts but in a far more conclusive way by the thousands of tablets found in its royal archive. The sheer volume of Ebla's tablets is difficult to appreciate. In fact those thousands of tablets have literally quadrupled the number of texts that date from the third millennium and before from every site previously excavated in the Middle East! When these texts are published and studied, there is no doubt that our knowledge about the beginnings of human achievement in areas such as science and mathematics, law and religion will increase dramatically. These tablets, many of which deal with the basic components of an urban society such as political and economic affairs, will illuminate our understanding of how urbanization first began and how the urban dwellers of antiquity maintained themselves. A good number of tablets describe Ebla's relationships with other urban centers in Syria and Mesopotamia. Certainly study of these will clarify the process of development through the blending of different cultural traditions. Of course, the importance of such studies for our own self-understanding is clear since our contemporary culture is ultimately rooted in these ancient cultures of the Near East.

Besides the importance of the Ebla tablets in revising our general understanding of the cultural process in the ancient Near East, they can provide the kind of detailed information which historians covet. For example, Pettinato has translated a text which he calls a "war bulletin" (see his *Archives of Ebla,* pp. 99–102). This text describes a battle fought between Ebla and its arch-rival Mari. Iblul, the leader of the enemy troops, is called "king of Mari and Assur." It was known that the cities of Mari and Assur became allies at one point in their history. However this alliance was always believed to have been the work of Shamshi-Adad I of Assyria who reigned in the nineteenth century B.C. The Ebla text which Pettinato has published demonstrates that the alliance was in force for some seven hundred years earlier than previously thought. This is the kind of significant revision of historical data that historians appreciate. The value of the Ebla tablets lies in such corrections and refinements of our knowledge rather than in some supposed connections with the Bible whose first words were written more than one thousand years after the fall of Ebla in 2275 B.C.

Because Ebla will add significantly to our knowledge of the third millennium, we can expect much more precision in the accounts of the culture of that period. When little data are available, the portrait of a given culture is quite uniform and rigid. The more data that can be studied, the more a given region will appear to be culturally varied and heterogeneous. Similarly such an explosion of knowledge will enable us to appreciate Ebla and the rest of the ancient Near Eastern cultures for their original contributions to the human endeavor. Too often these ancient cultures are seen merely as preparatory stages for other "more important" civilizations. The biblical scholar is tempted to portray the civilizations of the ancient Near East as simply the context within which ancient Israel received divine revelation. The classicist sees these ancient cultures as forerunners of Western civilization which properly begins with Greece and Rome. Ebla will help move the culture of the ancient Near East from the background to the center stage in our quest for understanding our cultural heritage.

Conclusion

What most people want to know about any archaeological work done in the Middle East is how it relates to the Bible. This preoccupation with the Bible is understandable on many counts, yet Ebla is important in its own right. When the full extent of Ebla's contributions is clear, we will see that much of its legacy has come down to us independently of the Bible. To look at the Ebla texts with one eye and the Bible with the other will cause the kind of distortions that make it difficult to increase our knowledge and appreciation of both. Such a distorted perspective makes it difficult to recognize the cultural gifts that are ours from an ancient people who created a thriving and important urban center almost five thousand years ago. Ebla's culture needs to be studied and appreciated for its own unique value before it is legitimate to make even the most tentative connections with the biblical tradition. The exact definition of Ebla's contribution will become more clear as archaeologists, linguists, historians and other scholars read to us the words written by our cultural ancestors so very long ago.

4
Jerusalem—David's City

Certainly no other city is more inviting and captivating to the biblical archaeologist than Jerusalem. Projects of one sort or another, some official and others unofficial, are constantly going forward in the city. Of the projects currently in progress, one of the most promising is the excavations of the Ophel Hill just outside the walls of the Old City. The Ophel attracted human occupation as far back as the Chalcolithic Period (4300–3300 B.C.). When the Israelite tribes were entering Canaan, the city on the Ophel was inhabited by the Jebusites whom the Israelites were unable to dislodge. Jerusalem was finally conquered by David who made the city his capital. David also moved the ark of the covenant to Jerusalem and his son Solomon built a temple in the city to house the ark. The presence of Solomon's temple in Jerusalem insured that this city would become a "holy city." In the centuries that followed, Jerusalem also became a holy place for Christianity and Islam as well as for Judaism. It is the sacred character of Jerusalem in the eyes of many believers that makes archaeological work in the city quite an issue. In 1977 Yigal Shiloh, a young Israeli archaeologist from Jerusalem's Hebrew University, accepted the challenge to excavate Jerusalem's Ophel Hill which was the site of David's city.

The Site

Many visitors to Jerusalem are shocked to learn that the walled "Old City" is relatively modern. The Old City's walls and gates, its

winding and narrow streets, its vaulted archways and the temple
mount all seem to transport the visitor back to the days of David and
Solomon. Actually the walls of the Old City were built by an Otto-
man sultan named Suleiman the Magnificent in the sixteenth century
A.D. The pattern of the city's streets follows that of the Roman city
built more than one hundred and fifty years after the death of Jesus.
All that remains of the Solomonic period within the walls is the
southeastern corner of the city which is the site of the beautiful Mos-
lem shrine called *Haram esh-Sharif* (the Noble Sanctuary). The
Haram contains two magnificent mosques and a number of small
monuments which were erected beginning in the seventh century
A.D. This third holiest of Islamic shrines is located atop the artificial
platform first erected by Solomon in the tenth century B.C. to provide a setting for the temple he built. The size of the present platform
is due to the renovation and enlargement of the temple and its environs undertaken by Herod the Great in the first century B.C. David
did not live in what is now known as the Old City. He lived in an
area which is actually outside the present walled city—some seventy-
five meters south of the temple mount.

The Jerusalem of David's time was built on the crest and slopes
of a small hill called Ophel. It is bounded on the east by the Kidron
Valley and on the west by the Hinnom Valley. These two meet at the
southern tip of the hill so that the Ophel is surrounded by steep
slopes on three sides. There is evidence of human habitation in this
area as far back as five thousand years ago. People were drawn to the
Ophel by the nearby Gihon spring which provided a reliable and
steady supply of water, by the easily defensible position of the hill
and by the fertility of the valleys below. The pre-Israelite settlement
on the Ophel was never really large. A population of six thousand
was crammed into twelve acres. However, the importance of the city
was not based on its size and population but on its geographical position. Jerusalem was located on the major lines of communication between north and south as well as between east and west in Canaan.
The Israelite tribes recognized Jerusalem's importance and tried to
take the city during the early years of their settlement in Canaan.
Apparently they had some initial success (Jgs 1:8), but if the Israelites did capture the city, it was soon lost again (Jos 15:63). The Canaanite settlement at Jerusalem probably prevented the Israelite

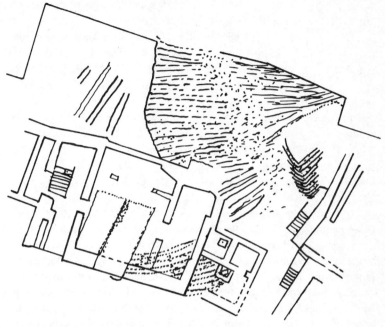

General Plan of the structures
in the City of David, from the Late Bronze Age to Roman times.

tribes from developing a genuine sense of unity. David's conquest of Jerusalem (2 Sam 5:6–10) made it possible for him to forge a united people from disparate tribes. Unfortunately David's achievement did not outlive him for very long, since the Davidic kingdom broke up after the death of David's son and successor Solomon. But the city's importance was assured because of the temple which Solomon built to house the ark of the covenant, the sign of God's presence in Israel's midst.

The passion which tied the people of ancient Israel to Jerusalem is clear enough: "If I forget you, Jerusalem, let my right hand wither. Let my tongue cleave to my palate if I do not remember you, if I do not set Jerusalem above my highest joy" (Ps 137:5–6). Christians too revere Jerusalem because it was the scene of Christ's death and resurrection as well as of the Church's beginnings. Moslems come to pray in Jerusalem because they believe the prophet Mohammed ascended to heaven from the city. No other place in the world is the focus of so many conflicting emotions, beliefs and hopes. All this makes Jerusalem both the best and the worst place to dig.

Every archaeologist who wishes to dig in Jerusalem has to contend with the emotions of religious people who live in the city. These emotions can be aroused very easily. In 1911 Montague Parker found out how deep feelings about Jerusalem really were. Parker's project in Jerusalem was more a quest for "treasure" than it was a genuine archaeological investigation. Rumors about Parker's work spread among the Arab populace which rioted in order to stop his work. For his own safety Parker had to be smuggled out of Palestine in a private boat in order to get back to England. The Ophel project under Shiloh's direction is a legitimate project led by a competent archaeologist with the approval of the Israeli government, yet Shiloh too has run afoul of some of the city's ultra-orthodox Jews. Some of these people claimed to have spotted human bones on the site of dig's operations, and stories quickly spread that the excavations at the Ophel were disturbing ancient burials. Israeli law forbids the disturbance of any burials by archaeological projects. This law was enacted at the request of the orthodox Jews who consider such disturbance to be a sacrilege. When Shiloh continued to dig, hundreds of protesters converged on the site to shut it down. The highest rabbinical authorities in Israel decreed that work at the Ophel had to cease. Passions were enflamed and the protests became violent. The matter ended up in the Israeli High Court of Justice which ruled in favor of Shiloh since there was no real evidence that any burials were disturbed by the excavation project. This did not settle the matter because many of the ultra-orthodox Jews do not accept the authority of the courts to adjudicate what they believe is a religious question. The work must proceed cautiously and in a way that will not offend anyone's religious sensibilities.

Shiloh had to face other practical problems as he began his work. First Jerusalem is a living city and its inhabitants cannot be summarily uprooted so that archaeologists can dig. The heavily built crest of the Ophel could not be excavated. Two plots of government owned land on the eastern slope of the hill were the site of the initial excavations. Secondly, earlier excavations on the hill uncovered no significant finds from the First Temple period (tenth to sixth centuries B.C.). In the opinion of some this did not bode well for Shiloh's project. There was some hesitation about initiating a new project at the Ophel, but circumstances converged in such a way as to make further work on the hill both possible and even necessary. The municipal government of Jerusalem began a construction project to modernize the drainage system in the Kidron Valley. In the course of the construction work, evidence of an ancient settlement was found, and archaeologists had to be called in to do salvage work so that these remains would not be bulldozed into dust. Secondly, the dumps of previous projects had to be removed since they began collapsing. Six children died in a landslide caused by one of these collapses. Quick action had to be taken in order to remove the dumps.

Yigal Shiloh agreed to lead a team which would excavate on the Ophel hill. Among Shiloh's goals were the exploration of the Canaanite and Israelite cities which had always eluded previous excavators, the clarification of ancient Jerusalem's complicated water system, and an understanding of the construction projects that were undertaken in the time of Solomon and Hezekiah as well as during the Persian period (sixth to fourth centuries B.C.). There was no lack of questions that needed answers. Shiloh hoped that the answers were to be found below the debris and dumps that hid David's city on the Ophel Hill.

The Millo

The Ophel project under Shiloh's direction is just the most recent in a series of excavations on the site. Even in the years of archaeology's infancy, it was realized that David's city was to be found south of the present Old City. The first archaeological project at the Ophel began in 1867. Despite the attention paid to this site since that date, very little of its architectural history was known until the excavations carried out between 1961 and 1967 by the British School of Archaeology under the direction of Kathleen Kenyon. One of the principal contributions of Kenyon's work was to describe the area of David's city by locating its walls. Kenyon had also thought that she had solved the problem of the enigmatic Hebrew word *millo* which is used to describe some architectural feature of David's city (cf. 2 Sam

5:9; 1 Kgs 9:15, 24; 11:27; 1 Chr 11:8; 2 Chr 32:5). Kenyon cut a deep trench into the eastern slope of the Ophel. This revealed architectural terracing which had collapsed in the sixth century B.C. probably during the Babylonian destruction of the city. Since that time these terraces were hidden by an immense pile of debris. Of course, architectural terracing is a practical necessity in any settlement built on the side of a hill as David's city was. When Kenyon found clear evidence of such terracing which would have supported the buildings erected on the Ophel, she identified this terracing as the *millo* of the Bible.

Kenyon's proposal was an attractive one. After all, the word *millo* probably means "filling," and these terraces were revetments of ten meters in height filled with stones, soil and rubble. These terraces provided flat and stable platforms for any building constructed on the steep terrain of the Ophel. Before Kenyon's find, many interpreters did not know what to make of the term *millo*, though most assumed that it referred to some aspect of Jerusalem's defenses. Though Kenyon's suggestion was welcomed by most scholars, there was an important demur from Lawrence Stager who suggested that what Kenyon found was a portion of the *shadmot qidron* (2 Kgs 23:4—"the slopes of the Kidron": NAB). The word *shadmot* refers to agricultural terraces in both Hebrew and Ugaritic, and Stager assumes that this word was also used to describe architectural terraces which were developments of earlier agricultural techniques. Stager also notes that to the observer looking at Jerusalem from the Kidron Valley, the city would have looked like a series of steps (terraces) with houses and gardens perched on each step. This explains the name "the slopes of the Kidron."

According to 2 Kings 23, King Josiah had various appurtenances of foreign cults removed from the Temple. He ordered these to be burned on the "slopes of the Kidron" outside Jerusalem. Stager notes that Kenyon found evidences of these terraces both inside and outside the walls of the city on the Ophel. The destruction of these objects from a foreign cult took place in a portion of the terraces located outside the city walls.

If Kenyon's terraces are not the *millo,* what is? Stager himself suggests that Shiloh may have come upon it in the course of his work on the Ophel. Working closer to the crest of the hill, Shiloh uncovered a magnificent five-story-high stone structure which may be a candidate for the biblical *millo*. The top of this structure was first uncovered by R. A. Macalister in the 1920's. Kenyon excavated a portion of the structure but did not completely expose it. On the basis of this partial excavation, she dated the structure to the Hasmonean Period (second century B.C.), which obviously eliminated it from being the *millo*. Shiloh was able to excavate this structure more completely and suggests that what Kenyon dated to the Hasmonean Period was merely the stone tower associated with the massive, tall, stepped-stone structure which is much earlier and may have been part of the substructure of David's city. Shiloh claims that it is the most monumental of all Israelite period structures found anywhere. Associated artifacts date the structure to the tenth century B.C. In the eighth century houses were built into its midsection but the original use of this construction may have been to support buildings erected in the course of the projects sponsored by David and Solomon. Though Shiloh has not completed his study of this structure, he believes that it was a portion of the earliest defense system which protected the royal precincts of Jerusalem. Thus this structure would have marked the extent of the royal enclave of the city. Shiloh himself is not ready to identify this structure as the *millo*. He believes that more excavation is necessary to be certain about the identity and function of this structure and its relation to the other architectural features which the Bible mentions as part of David's city.

The Water System

A very exciting and important activity of Shiloh's project has been the effort to clarify the complex system of tunnels, shafts and channels which make up the water system of ancient Jerusalem. The Gihon spring at the foot of the Ophel provided the city with a steady supply of water, and certainly that is what drew the earliest inhabitants to this hill. Once a city developed on the Ophel, a system had to be developed in order to insure an efficient distribution of water, especially in time of war. Perhaps nothing is more important in understanding how an ancient city worked than to know how its water system functioned. A system that was able to deliver water in time of war was absolutely necessary in withstanding a siege operation, especially in the hot and dry climate of Palestine.

Archaeologists already knew of three separate systems which were operative in ancient Jerusalem. The best known was Hezekiah's Tunnel, so named after the king who ordered its excavation to insure the city's water supply during the Assyrian crisis in the eighth century B.C. The Bible alludes to this project in 2 Kings 20:20, 2 Chronicles 32:30, and Isaiah 22:8–11. The workmen who actually carved this conduit out of solid rock left an inscription in the tunnel. The inscription describes their method of operation: two teams, one at the spring and the other at the foot of the hill, hacked away at the limestone until they cleared a channel and met to connect the portion of the channel which each team cleared. This project saved the city's water supply and probably helped Jerusalem withstand the Assyrian onslaught that threatened its very existence.

A second system was the Siloam channel which has been excavated by Raymond Weill in the early part of this century. Shiloh re-excavated a portion of the channel which courses both above and below ground. The channel was intended to serve as an irrigation system for the city's outlying fields. Water entered the channel from the Gihon spring. At various intervals a "window" was cut into the side of the channel. This allowed the water to be directed from the channel to the fields where it was needed. Shiloh believes that the channel also provided a drainage system for the city.

The third system was made of a shaft and a complex of tunnels known collectively as Warren's Shaft. It was named after Charles Warren who discovered it in 1867. It was an ingenious system made up of a wide tunnel whose entrance was inside the city wall. This first tunnel sloped downward and extended for about fourteen meters. It led to a second horizontal tunnel of twenty-nine meters. At the end of this second tunnel there was a vertical shaft of thirteen meters where water from the Gihon spring could be drawn by Jerusalemites who would be protected from attack by the walls of the tunnel. Before Shiloh's excavations it was generally accepted that these three systems operated at different times in Jerusalem's history. Warren's Shaft was presumed to be the oldest of the three—dating to the Canaanite period. Some believe that this shaft was used by David's soldiers to enter Jerusalem to take it from the Jebusites (cf. 2 Sam 5:8). There is no evidence supporting this hypothesis. The height of the shaft and the skill it takes to surmount its height make this very unlikely. The Siloam channel supposedly dated to the Solomonic period while Hezekiah's tunnel was built in the eighth century. It was assumed that each successive system was designed to replace its predecessor.

Hezekiah's tunnel remained open and in fact had become a popular tourist attraction, but the other two systems became covered up with the debris from earlier excavations. Clearing a portion of the Siloam irrigation channel proved an easy task in comparison with clearing Warren's Shaft which had become clogged with debris and silt of a century. Shiloh had to employ alpine climbers to scale the sheer vertical shaft. They were able to erect equipment which permitted others to reach the top of the shaft and begin clearing operations. Shiloh also felt it necessary to contract with South African mining engineers in order to insure that the horizontal tunnels could be cleared without any danger to the excavators or damage to the structure itself. Clearing these tunnels proved to be an exhausting and time-consuming task but once the excavation was complete, Shiloh was prepared to offer an alternative suggestion regarding the relationship of the three systems to one another.

Shiloh is sure that Warren's Shaft was used as late as the Herodian Period (first century B.C.). He bases this conclusion on the architecture of the entry tunnel and the vaulted chambers which were added to an earlier entry way in order to protect those who used the shaft from falling debris. The barrel vault of these added structures is unknown prior to the first centrury B.C. This means that Warren's Shaft could have been in use until the Roman destruction of Jerusalem in A.D. 70. The three systems then probably functioned in complementary ways. Warren's Shaft, the earliest of the three, provided a convenient and safe access to water in time of both peace and war. The Siloam channel facilitated the irrigation of cultivated areas outside the city walls as well as the storage of water in reservoirs in the eastern part of the city. Hezekiah's Tunnel was added in the eighth century to carry water from the spring to a pool within the city walls

on the southwestern side of the city. Thus each of the systems ful-
filled a separate purpose in making urban life on the Ophel a genuine
possibility, for without water there could be no Jerusalem.

Other Finds

Shiloh's excavations on the Ophel uncovered a number of well-
preserved four-room houses which date to the pre-Exilic period. The
walls of these houses were plastered and were preserved to a height
of three meters. The floor plan was rather uniform: there were three
oblong rooms in a row with a fourth room running at right angles
along the back. The inner room usually contained an oven and obviously served as the food-preparation area. One house had a small
stone fashioned into what looked like a toilet seat set into the plaster
floor. Nearby was a wash basin. The houses were built one upon another on terracing erected to support these buildings on the slopes of
the Ophel. David's city probably was not much larger than that of its
Canaanite predecessor since David's Jerusalem was confined to the
Ophel. In the centuries which followed the city did expand in area
and population, but in David's time the city did not grow much beyond the dimensions it had in the Jebusite period. The streets of the
city were winding and narrow since they had to follow the contours
of the hill. The close quarters meant that privacy was out of the question. The people of Jerusalem literally lived on top of each other on
the architectural terracing that made it possible to live on the slopes
of the Ophel.

Other finds made by Shiloh's excavators include the remnants
of an Iron Age wall built by the pre-Israelite inhabitants of Jerusalem, the reinforcements of the city's defenses from the eighth century
B.C. when Hezekiah had to face the Assyrians (cf. 2 Kgs 18:1–20:21)
and a post-exilic fortification system built atop the destruction layer
left by the Babylonian sack of Jerusalem in 587 B.C. The artifacts
found at the Ophel are quite diverse and reflect a picture of material
prosperity. Shiloh reports an abundance of finds of all types: pottery,
coins, lithic objects, glass, bone utensils and metallic objects. Some of
the ceramic materials is stamped or bears inscriptions. Jar handles
from the eighth to seventh centuries are stamped with the words "to
the king," indicating that the jars contained provisions belonging to

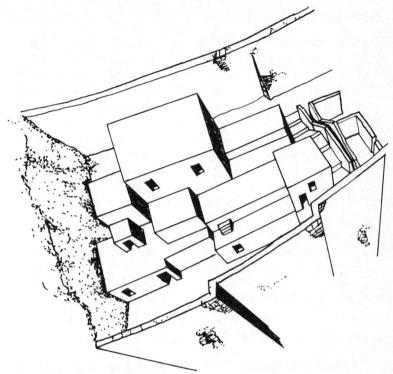

Drawing of houses behind the city walls of the City of David.

the palace. Some of the pottery dating from the Persian period (sixth century B.C.) is stamped with the word "Judah" which was the name of the territory to which David's large empire had been reduced. Jar handles from the Hellenistic Period (fourth to second century B.C.) are stamped with the word Jerusalem. Some individual pieces of pottery were found to bear the names of various individuals, e.g., a jug from the seventh century B.C. bore the inscription "Ahiel." Finally a large stone plaque fragment was found with a three-line inscription incised on it with a chisel. The eighth century inscription is fragmentary but it seems to commemorate the construction of a building used to store large amounts of property belonging to the royal house.

The Archaeological Park

The excavations at the Ophel are not completed, but the project is not limited to excavation alone. When the archaeological work is completed the site will be transformed into a public park. Shiloh and his volunteers then are very concerned about the restoration and maintenance of the city walls, the houses, the water system, the massive unidentified structure and whatever else may be uncovered in the digging seasons that lie ahead. There are a number of such parks already in existence at sites previously excavated, such as Caesarea Martima, Hazor, Masada, and Megiddo among others. The park that will be constructed at the Ophel will provide students, tourists and all those interested in archaeology with a chance to admire not only the work of twentieth century excavators but the ancient architects and engineers who built Jerusalem. What will make the Ophel park unique is that it will be located in the heart of a living city which attracts visitors from around the world. This park is destined to be enjoyed by weekend strollers as well as by the scholars and pilgrims drawn to the Holy City.

Conclusion

Because Jerusalem is considered "holy" by so many people of different religious traditions, excavation at the Ophel has been and will continue to be a very delicate matter. Religious sensibilities are easily aroused. Though Shiloh has encountered some vocal opposition and even some violent demonstrations, he has been able to carry on with the help of the Israeli High Court of Justice. In a similar vein, because Jerusalem is so important for so many people, excavations there are news. Again this causes problems for archaeologists since journalists with little or no archaeological background will visit the site for only a few hours yet are not hesitant to sensationalize the work of the archaeologist beyond recognition. Because Jerusalem has been a magnet drawing archaeologists for over a century to its remains from antiquity, Shiloh had to dig through the dumps of his predecessors. He also had to face the very practical problem of trying to excavate the side of a hill located in the middle of a large city which is full of tourists throughout the year. Despite these and the other kinds of practical problems that face archaeologists, the Ophel dig has been quite successful up to the present. It is well managed and offers the promise of continued careful excavation and prompt publication. In spite of all his headaches over the Ophel, Shiloh would not trade places with any of his colleagues. Jerusalem can be one of the worst places to dig but it is also one of the best places.

5

Capernaum—The City of Jesus

Capernaum is a town located on the northwestern shore of the Sea of Galilee. The Gospel of Matthew states that Jesus moved from Nazareth to Capernaum when he began his ministry (Mt 4:13). Such a move is quite understandable since Nazareth was an unimportant village with a very small population (cf. Jn 1:46) while Capernaum was a relatively large town with a population approaching fifteen thousand. This was large enough to make Capernaum a center for the collection of taxes (Mk 2:14). Capernaum is mentioned sixteen times in the New Testament—all of these occurrences are in the Gospels which present the town as the hub of Jesus' Galilean ministry. While Matthew simply states that Jesus traveled throughout Galilee to teach in its synagogues (4:23), Mark mentions the synagogue of Capernaum by name as one of the places where Jesus taught (1:21). The other two evangelists are even more specific. Luke identifies the synagogue of Capernaum as the site of an exorcism performed by Jesus (4:31–37) and John names the same synagogue as the location of Jesus' discourse on the bread of life (6:59). John notes that the reaction to this discourse on the part of many of the disciples was quite negative and it became the cause of their defection (6:60, 66). According to Matthew (11:23–24) and Luke (10:15), Jesus cursed Capernaum. What precipitated this act was the town's resistance to Jesus' call for repentance. But no matter what the people's reaction to Jesus was, the town was an important locus of Jesus' activity.

The original Semitic name of the town means "the village of Nahum." Since the town is never mentioned in the Hebrew Scriptures, it is doubtful that this "Nahum" was the ancient Israelite prophet. Most probably the town was named after the original owner of the land on which the town was built. Medieval Jewish sources do associate Capernaum with the prophet Nahum, but this identification is without any historical basis. The first century Jewish historian Josephus wrote that he was brought to Capernaum after being wounded in the course of the first revolt against Rome. Talmudic sources relate that a Christian community existed there by the second century. Finally Egeria, a Christian pilgrim of the late fourth century, mentions visiting this site in the course of her travels. The town was rather prosperous because it was a center for trade and commerce with regions to the north and east of Galilee. Capernaum was destroyed in the seventh century and was never rebuilt, though a thirteenth century writer notes that a few poor fishermen and their families lived there.

Archaeological study of this site began in 1838 when Edward Robinson surveyed the ruins at Capernaum and correctly identified the exposed architectural fragments as belonging to a synagogue. Charles Wilson of London's Palestine Exploration Fund began a small-scale excavation at the site in 1866. He was the first to identify the site as Capernaum and concluded that the synagogue he surveyed was the very one built by a Roman centurion (Lk 7:5) and the one in which Jesus preached. Additional work on the site was done by H. H. Kitchener in 1881. The activity of these foreign archaeologists at Capernaum prompted some of the local populace to begin looking for treasure or at least some small artifacts to sell on the local antiquities market. Also local contractors began looting the site for stones to be used in their construction projects. Fortunately this was stopped once the site was acquired by the Franciscan Order in 1894. The friars who remain custodians of the site until the present took very practical steps to insure that there would be no more looting of the site. Among these was the construction of a high wall around the property.

The solicitude of the Franciscans made continued archaeological study of the site a possibility. Additional work on the synagogue was done by H. Kohl and C. Watzinger in 1905 as part of their important survey of the synagogues of Galilee. From 1905 until 1926

two Franciscans continued excavations. Both Wendelin Hinter-
keuser and Gaudentius Orfali began digging in the synagogue area
but they extended their soundings and came upon an octagonal
structure south of the synagogue. Despite this new discovery, the
synagogue remained the center of activity. Under Fr. Orfali work began on the reconstruction of the synagogue. The good number of architectural fragments which remained from the destroyed building
made it possible to begin modest attempts to restore the synagogue—
a project which is still in progress. Recent excavations began in 1968
and continued until 1972 under the direction of Franciscans Virgilio
Corbo and Stanislao Loffreda. Though a final report of four volumes
was published by Corbo and Lofredda, work continues on the synagogue and Fr. Corbo promises another volume stating his final conclusions about the building.

The Synagogue

The obvious place to begin a description of the archaeological
discoveries at Capernaum is the synagogue. Not only was this building the primary focus of excavations in recent years but also it must
have been a very impressive structure in antiquity. The present par-
tially reconstructed state of the building makes even the casual observer marvel. Its original state was certainly breathtaking in its
beauty. The building was constructed of large white limestone ashlars (rectangular blocks of hewn stone). Their external surfaces were
polished in order to imitate the appearance of marble. The white
limestone ashlars served to make the building stand out in contrast
to most of the other structures of the town which were built using
the basalt (a black volcanic rock) which is native to the area immediately surrounding Capernaum. The builders of the synagogue had to
import the limestone from neighboring areas at some expense. This
together with the intricate decorative motifs in the building's architectural components shows that the erection of this synagogue was
an expensive project. That Capernaum was able to underwrite such a
project is an indication of the community's economic status. The
ashlars were set without mortar and their interior surfaces were left
rough in order to receive plaster. The floor of the synagogue was
made of stone pavers. The building measures about 24.5 × 18.5 me-

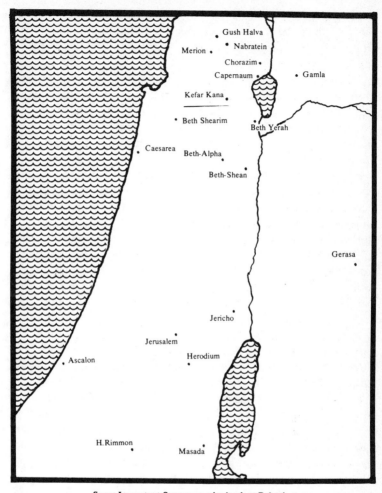

Some Important Synagogues in Ancient Palestine

ters. Adjoining the synagogue to the east was a courtyard with a portico covered on three sides. The courtyard measures approximately 20.4 × 13.3 meters. Unlike the synagogue it was not perfectly rectangular in shape but trapezoidal. The courtyard and its portico provided open space as well as a shaded area outside the worship space for all the diverse activities that normally took place in the environs of the synagogue. For example, this area would have been used for study, trying of legal cases, communal meals and simple social gatherings. This extra feature is another indication of the extravagance which marked this building.

Despite the looting of the site in the last century before the Franciscans took custody of it, architectural fragments of the synagogue were so numerous as to make possible a hypothetical reconstruction of the building's appearance. One place to begin is with the facade. The building's front wall is oriented toward the south, i.e., toward Jerusalem. Eight other early synagogues in Palestine orient themselves to Jerusalem in this manner. In eighteen others, the internal architecture of the building is arranged so that the worshipers faced Jerusalem during prayer. Rabbinic law mandated such an arrangement in accordance with the biblical tradition that prayers be offered while the worshiper is facing into the direction of the temple (cf. 1 Kgs 8:44 and 2 Chr 6:34, 38). A few synagogues face the east in accordance with a disputed Talmudic injunction that a synagogue's entrance, like that of the temple, must face east.

The facade of Capernaum's synagogue can be divided into three fields: the lower story, the upper story and the gabled roof. The lower story was marked by three elaborately decorated doorways. The lintels of these doorways bear carvings of date palms and other fruits of the land, shell motifs, garlands, geometric patterns and animal figures. The latter were defaced probably by iconoclasts who objected to any representations of living creatures. Similar defacing is in evidence throughout Palestine and is often associated with the Islamic incursions into the area beginning in the seventh century since Islam forbids representational art. A cornice which itself is rich in moldings of various floral and geometric patterns separates the first and second stories of the facade. The central feature of the second story was a large arch above the central doorway. This arch framed a window which allowed sunlight to enter the building. On either side of the large central window was a smaller window. Each of these two windows was fashioned to resemble the facade of a temple: two small columns supported a gable with a shell-motif in the center. A second cornice which was even more highly decorated than the first separated the second story from the gables. The roof was probably covered with roofing tiles.

The three entrances of the facade opened to the interior of the synagogue which was arranged in the style of the Greco-Roman basilica. The distinctive feature of the basilical style of interior architecture was two rows of columns which divided the interior space of the building into a central nave and two side aisles. In Capernaum this nave was 8.34 meters wide and the aisles were 3.56 meters wide. This building also contained a third row of columns which served to close the two rows of columns at the north end of the building. This third row created another aisle which was 8.38 meters wide. The builders of twenty-three ancient synagogues in Palestine adopted the basilical form from the Romans and modified it to serve the religious needs of the Jewish community which met regularly for prayer and study. Along the interior walls of the synagogue were two rows of benches for use by the elderly and others of frail health during the service. All others would simply sit on mats placed on the floor. In the southwest corner of the synagogue, a feature of the upper row of benches appears to have been the "Chair of Moses" used by the leader of the synagogue (cf. Mt 23:2). Precise identification of this feature is not possible due to its fragmentary state. A similar "chair" was found in the synagogue of the nearby village of Chorazin.

A good number of columns survived the looting and have been incorporated into the reconstruction of the synagogue. The bases of the columns were of the Attic type (marked by simplicity) while the capitals were of the Corinthian type (marked by highly ornate decorations). Some of the capitals were adorned with recognizable Jewish symbols: the *menorah* (the seven-branched candlestick), the *shofar* (the ram's horn) and an incense shovel. These implements were used in the temple. Two of the columns bear inscriptions. One is in Greek, the other in Aramaic. Both name individuals who "built" the particular column. The individuals named on the columns were probably not those who fabricated the columns themselves but were rather benefactors who financed their erection. This may indicate that the synagogue was built in some part by public subscription.

One other feature of the synagogue's internal architecture that calls for comment is the frieze, the decorative limestone beam which connects the tops of the columns that make up the lateral row along the north end of the synagogue. The central feature of the frieze is the side-view of a wheeled carriage which served as a portable Torah

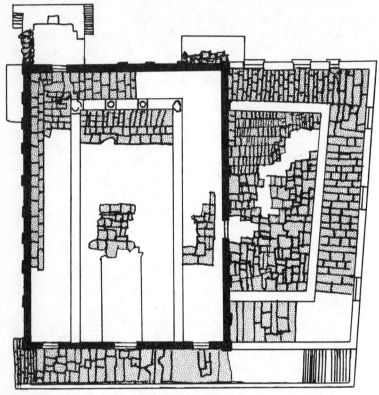

Plan of Capernaum synagogue

shrine for the storage of the holy scrolls read during the service. The shrine is made to look like an Ionic temple with double-winged doors, above which is a scalloped shell. The roof is gabled. Other figures on the frieze include two eagles and a goat. The latter may represent the sign of Capricorn from the zodiac. The zodiac was used in a number of ancient synagogues as a decorative motif. The animal figures on the frieze are the only ones from the synagogue which escaped the hands of the iconoclasts. Two features of the synagogue's internal architecture have not been adequately explained to everyone's satisfaction. A number of small columns and capitals as well as other architectural fragments have led some archaeologists to conclude that there was a second story to the building which served as the women's gallery. Loffreda maintains that the building's foundations could not hold a second story. In any case, the separation of men and women in Jewish worship probably occurred somewhat later than the period when Capernaum's synagogue was in use. The second unexplained feature of the synagogue's interior is the pair of platforms which were built on either side of the main entrance. Corbo simply describes these in his report on the building without suggesting what their use may have been. J. Strange who reviewed Corbo's reports offers the suggestion that these platforms were built to support two *aediculae* (small shrines). One of these shrines would have been the holy ark which housed the scrolls read in the worship service; the other could have housed the *menorah* which became a standard element of a synagogue's appointments. If this hypothesis is correct, the location of these *aediculae* along the southern wall of the building would compel the worshiper to turn around after entering the building from the south. Thus the prayers of the community would be offered while facing Jerusalem in accord with biblical and rabbinic prescriptions.

Although there are some disagreements regarding the interpretation of certain elements of the synagogue's internal architecture such as the role of the platforms discussed above, certainly the most controversial aspect of the reports that Corbo and Loffreda produced after their excavations at Capernaum concerns the dating they propose for the building. They have concluded that Capernaum's synagogue was built between A.D. 350–450. Some of the early excavators of the synagogue such as Wilson and Orfali dated the building to the first century. Fr. Orfali was confident that he had uncovered the very building in which Jesus preached and worked miracles. Today all reputable archaeologists are united in their rejection of a first century date for the synagogue. This does not mean that no synagogue existed in Capernaum in the first century, but simply that none has been located up to this point. In all probability, the building in which Jesus preached was located in the same general area as the present synagogue since communities generally did not relocate their synagogues. Whatever expansion or reconstruction was necessary would be done on the very same site. There have been soundings below the foundations of the present building. Apparently the structures that are there were private homes. One of these may have been used as the community's synagogue in Jesus' day.

After their excavations at Capernaum in 1905, Kohl and Watzinger suggested that the building was erected in the second century—a date which has been accepted by most archaeologists who find a fourth century date astonishingly late. Corbo and Loffreda began their work with a second to third century date for the synagogue as a working hypothesis, but by the end of their excavations they were convinced that the building could be dated no earlier than the middle of the fourth century. Corbo and Loffreda admit that they were unprepared for this conclusion. The evidence that led them to it caught them completely by surprise. Archaeologists sometimes do have to discard their working hypothesis in the course of their excavations. The real answers in archaeology lie below the surface of the ground. When excavation reveals them, archaeologists must accept the evidence before them and reformulate their hypothesis when necessary.

Corbo and Loffreda began by sinking seven trenches: two within the synagogue, one in the courtyard and three in an area outside but immediately adjacent to the synagogue and one somewhat southeast of the synagogue. Their first important discovery was that the synagogue was not built on virgin soil but on debris from previous occupations. This supported an artificial platform on which the synagogue was built. Obviously the synagogue was at the very least the third and most recent structure on the site where it stands. Identifying and dating the earlier structures would clearly make dating the synagogue easier and more credible. The earliest structures below the synagogue included stone pavers, walls, staircases, homes and a drainage system. The archaeologists called this urban area stratum A. The present synagogue rests upon what was once an area which was made up of a group of homes. Once it was decided to erect the present building on this site, this area was filled in with basalt stones, discarded pottery, ash and earth. This layer of fill made up stratum B. The fill layer was sealed with a layer of mortar (stratum C) with an average thickness of thirty centimeters. This created the artificial platform on which the synagogue was built. All this work was necessary to insure that the synagogue would be erected on the highest point of the town in accordance with the requirements found in rabbinic literature. The stone pavers of the synagogue and courtyard were laid while the mortar of stratum C was still soft, since the outline of some missing pavers was still discernible in the hardened mortar.

Each of these strata needed to be excavated separately so that each could be dated with some precision. Since stratum C was made up of a thick layer of mortar, it effectively sealed the two strata below, making the artifactual evidence of these strata an infallible guide in dating. The layer of mortar made it practically impossible for anything to intrude into strata A or B. What the excavators needed to do was to dig carefully so that no contamination would be introduced into these strata during the course of their excavations.

The evidence used by Corbo and Loffreda to date each of the three strata was primarily the coins they found in them. Coins are very helpful since they can usually be given an absolute date. Not all evidence from coins, however, is of equal value due to the different circumstances in which the coins came to be present in the strata. In some instances the coins may have been deliberately placed. Sometimes the architect of antiquity placed coins in the foundations of the structures which they were erecting as a votive offering. If it can be determined that a coin was deliberately placed in some structure, it is possible to get rather specific information about the date when the building was erected. Some coins were inadvertently lost in antiquity and therefore give only an approximate date with regard to the building's construction since the coins could have been lost at any time during that building's use. Finally whole caches of coins are sometimes discovered. Clearly these were hidden in antiquity for later recovery but for some reason were never recovered. In such a situation, the latest coin in the cache can provide the date after which the building's destruction took place but cannot give an absolute date for its construction since the cache could have been hidden at any point in the stratum's use. The excavators of Capernaum found coins in all three categories.

In stratum A (the urban area beneath the present synagogue), five coins were found. All of them were from the fourth century A.D. Since these coins were presumably accidental losses, they do not tell us when the houses of stratum A were built but they do force us to conclude that the synagogue could not have been erected in the second or third century. How could fourth century coins find their way to this stratum *after* the synagogue was built upon it? Loffreda acknowledges that at least one of the coins could have been introduced into stratum A during the course of the fill operations (stratum B) and that he found it difficult to make a clear distinction between the end of stratum A and the beginning of stratum B. Since the real concern of the excavation was to date the synagogue, these difficulties do not invalidate the conclusion that the building could not have been built prior to the fourth century.

The fill of stratum B contained coins from the fourth century B.C. to the second half of the fourth century A.D. These coins were probably lost in antiquity and not deliberately placed in the fill. The five latest coins are late fourth century A.D. coins, indicating that the fill material could not have been set in place any earlier than the date of these coins. Again this makes it impossible to date the synagogue which was built *above* the fill to the second or third century.

Stratum C yielded an unbelievable number of coins clustered in two hoards, one of which contained 2,290 coins and the other 6,000. The latter hoard was found sealed by the stone pavers of the synagogue's platform. Several of these coins were firmly embedded in the layer of mortar which constitutes this stratum and thereby indicate that they were placed there before the mortar hardened. The latest of these coins from the mortar dates to the middle of the fifth century. Clearly the mortar could not have been laid before that date. Late Roman period coins were also found in the foundation of the benches within the synagogue itself and in trenches outside the synagogue. Corbo and Loffreda felt compelled by this numismatic evidence coming from different stratigraphic contexts to date the synagogue building to the late fourth to early fifth century.

This new, late date for the Capernaum synagogue has touched off a flurry of controversy since it contradicts what has been up to now an accepted way to date synagogues through classification of their architectural type. According to this scheme, most archaeologists believed that the synagogue of Capernaum was the best example of an architectural style that flourished in Galilee during the second and third centuries of our era. This type has been called "early Galilean" and was characterized by an elaborate triple facade oriented toward Jerusalem. Its internal architecture was basilical and its floor was paved with stone slabs. Other features of the early Galilean synagogue include a second story which served as the women's gallery and benches along the inner walls. Apart from the women's gallery, this description of the "early Galilean" type fits the Capernaum synagogue perfectly. According to this same theory, synagogues built in the fourth century were "broadhouses." In these buildings the wall of orientation (the wall facing Jerusalem) was one of the longer or broader walls as opposed to the shorter end-walls of the basilical type. A third type of building supposedly flourished from the fifth to the eighth centuries and was known as the "apsidal" synagogue. This building type was similar to the basilical type except that an apse (a curved, semi-circular recess projecting from a building) was added to the wall opposite the entrance. The apsidal wall faced Jerusalem and was the focus of worship. Obviously the conclusion of Corbo and Loffredda upset this chronological classification of synagogue architecture since they suggest that a basilical structure was erected when supposedly basilicas were out of vogue.

Two of the archaeologists who cling to the second-third century date for the Capernaum synagogue, G. Foerster and M. Avi-Yonah, do not reject the data put forward by Corbo and Loffreda; they choose to interpret the numismatic evidence in another way. Foerster and Avi-Yonah maintain that the fourth century coins found in strata A and B were introduced there during renovations on the syn-

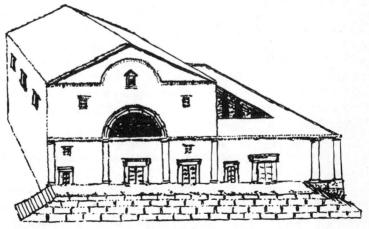

Reconstruction of Capernaum synagogue

agogue. In other words, they do not believe that the mortar layer (stratum C) sealed the layer beneath. Strata A and B were contaminated *in antiquity* during repairs on the building which they believe was erected in the second century. Avi-Yonah notes that the two coin hoards found in stratum C indicate that people were hiding these coins because they were afraid of attack and ruin. In such circumstances a major building project like the synagogue would not have been undertaken.

Both Foerster and Avi-Yonah insist that the numismatic evidence alone is not sufficient to support a hypothesis which dates the synagogue to the fourth century. They suggest testing the hypothesis against stylistic and historical evidence, i.e., testing the hypothesis according to the theory of synagogue types. Foerster notes the Capernaum synagogue represents a pattern in Roman architecture that is found throughout Syria and Asia Minor in the second century—a pattern which stresses the external appearance of a building. The architecture of the Byzantine period (fourth to seventh century) changes the focus to the interior space. For example, the lavish mosaics of the synagogue at the nearby site of Hamat Tiberias reflect the aesthetic concerns of the Byzantine period. According to Foerster it would be a mistake to group the Capernaum synagogue and its plain pavement slabs with the Hamat Tiberias synagogue with its ornate mosaic floor. If the Capernaum synagogue would have been built in the fourth century, it would have been an architectural anachronism in its own day. Finally Avi-Yonah considers it highly unlikely that a magnificent structure like the Capernaum synagogue could have been built in the fourth century since the emperors reigning at that time, Constantine and his son Constantius II, were quite hostile to the Jews. Foerster and Avi-Yonah consider a fourth century date for the Capernaum synagogue highly unlikely on stylistic and historical grounds.

Avi-Yonah himself suggests the way out of the difficulty caused by the imperial policy regarding the Jews. Byzantine authorities on the local level could be convinced by a large enough bribe to ignore official policy. Recent archaeological projects in Galilee have called into question the rigid historical typology that is behind objections to the fourth century date for the synagogue. Although Foerster and Avi-Yonah find it difficult to accept architectural diversity within

Galilee, this is precisely what various excavation projects have made clear was the case. It is apparent that the evolutionary concept of early (basilical), middle (broadhouse) and late (apsidal) forms for synagogue architecture is untenable. Architectural diversity is a simple reflection of religious diversity. In recent years the concept of a "normative" Judaism has been rejected in favor of a portrait of Judaism which is rich in its varied expressions. One of these varied expressions is religious architecture which reflects this ideological differentiation. In fact, the simple impulse to differentiate oneself from one's neighbors may be all the explanation necessary to appreciate the different architectural styles which are exhibited in the synagogues of Palestine. This does not mean that the excavators of Capernaum are above criticism regarding the date they assign to the synagogue. Final evaluation of their work will be put off until the publication of the volume on the synagogue which Corbo has promised. In addition more work will need to be done on stratum A (the urban area before the synagogue) in order to firmly establish its date before the debate about Capernaum's synagogue will end.

The most recent work on the Capernaum synagogue is a good commentary on an archaeological truism: "The answers lie below." Even though Corbo and Loffreda began their work fully expecting to find support for a second or third century date for the building, the evidence was simply not forthcoming. The coins which they did find in the strata below the synagogue compelled them to conclude that the Capernaum synagogue was built two hundred years later than had been generally assumed by scholars. Old ideas do not die easily, so there is still quite a debate regarding the interpretation of the data which Corbo and Loffreda use to support their late dating. In any case, those on both sides of the debate will have to agree that archaeology is a science whose conclusions must reflect the evidence uncovered in the course of excavations. When the evidence speaks, scholars must be ready to revise even their most cherished theories.

The Octagonal House

In addition to the synagogue at Capernaum, there is another large building at the site which Fr. Orfali uncovered during his excavations in the 1920's and which Fr. Corbo and Fr. Loffreda excavated during their recent project. Orfali noticed that the building was made up of three concentric octagons. The floor of the central octagon was paved with a very beautiful mosaic whose centerpiece was a peacock which in Christian iconography represents immortality. Orfali identified the building as a baptistry. He took his cue not only from the mosaic but from similar buildings that can be found in Italy where baptistries are sometimes free standing buildings. One of the most famous of these is the baptistry of the cathedral in Florence. Local guides intent on adding a bit more color to their commentaries described the octagonal building as "St. Peter's House" since the Gospel of Mark speaks about a house of Peter in Capernaum (1:21, 29–31). The building is clearly too ornate to have been the home of a first century fisherman. Less romantic suggestions regarding the original use of the octagonal structure considered it to be a public fountain or the remnants of a church.

When work began on the octagonal structure, Corbo and Loffreda noticed that the outermost of the octagons was not complete. Three of its sides were missing. Excavation of the other two octagons cleared up this mystery and served to confirm the hypothesis that the structure was indeed a church. The central octagon enclosed the worship space itself. It was in turn enclosed by a second octagon. To this second octagon was attached an apse and baptistry. This semicircular structure made it impossible to close off the third octagon. The discovery of the apse and baptistry made it clear that the octagonal structure was an ancient church building. The excavators date the building to the fifth century and maintain that it was constructed in two phases. The two inner octagons were built first. At a later time the baptistry was added to the second octagon and a third partial octagon enclosed the building.

The octagonal shape of the church is not unique. Other examples can be found from the fourth to fifth centuries. On the Mount of Olives there is just such a structure built over the spot venerated as the site of Jesus' ascension. Other examples are the original structures in Bethlehem built over the place associated with the nativity and in Jerusalem over the site of Jesus' tomb. Octagonal structures then are usually memorial churches which were erected on the site of special events. These churches did not serve local congregations but pilgrims. Perhaps at one time the church at Capernaum came to be used by a "parish" community, as may be indicated by the addition of the baptistry. At first, however, the building was a memorial church. But what memory was the building seeking to preserve? An obvious suggestion is the remembrance of Jesus' residence at Capernaum in the "house of Simon and Andrew" (Mk 1:29). Perhaps the local guides were not too far afield when they described the octagonal building to tourists. The next task faced by the excavators was to determine, if possible, what was memorialized by the church in Capernaum.

The excavators believe that they have found the answer. Corbo and Loffreda are convinced that the octagonal building is in fact a structure built over Peter's house. They maintain that their excavations have shown that a private home dating from the Early Roman Period (63 B.C.–A.D. 70) was rebuilt as a shrine by Christians who used the building until the fourth century. In the fifth century the octagonal building was erected over the site of the early Roman house. A short time later the apse and baptistry were added. This new structure continued in use until the seventh century Islamic invasion when Capernaum was abandoned.

The fourth century structure is significant because of the graffiti scratched on the wall presumably by the pilgrims who came to pray in the building. There are well over one hundred such graffiti written primarily in Greek with a few in Semitic languages (Aramaic, Syriac and Hebrew). There are two in Latin. Some of these graffiti are clearly confessional statements about Jesus which call him "Lord" or "Christ." This is evidence enough that the visitors to this building were Christians. Two of the inscriptions allegedly mention the name Peter. It is on the basis of these two that the excavators claim that the structure was once the house of Peter. Unfortunately the two graffiti in question are extremely difficult to decipher. At first glance, the inscription looks like a jumbled mass of lines. The trained epigrapher (an expert in deciphering ancient inscriptions and texts) can make something out but the evidence of the name Peter is certainly equivocal. In any case, even if the word Peter was written by some pilgrim there is nothing to indicate that the name referred to the apostle and was not simply the name of the pilgrim who was doing nothing more than leaving his name behind in the shrine. This is an impulse followed even today by visitors to historical sites.

While the presence of the name Peter among the graffiti is difficult to establish with certainty, excavation did clarify the history of
the structure on top of which the octagonal church was built. The
structure was originally built at the beginning of the Early Roman
Period (c. 63 B.C.). The building was of simple construction. Like
others in the Roman period it was a cluster of small rooms around a
courtyard. The stones used to make the walls were basalt which is
found throughout the region surrounding Capernaum. These stones
were not worked except where necessary around the doors of the
rooms. The walls were not of the size to support a second story or a
roof of masonry. The floor consisted of more basalt stones which
were not fitted too well so that there were large gaps between individual stones. The courtyard was the work and food preparation
area. An oven was found in the southwest corner of the courtyard.
The house is basically the same as the others which have been excavated in Capernaum.

In the middle of the first century A.D. the house underwent
some important modifications that indicate a change in its usage.
First of all, the largest room in the house had an arch built into it.
This arch permitted the roof to be higher and to consist of masonry
in place of the typical mud, straw and branches. Secondly, the floors,
walls and ceilings of the room were plastered. This does not seem to
have been the practice in Capernaum since no other private home
has been found to contain any evidence of plastering. The ceramic
evidence also points to a change in function for the house. Before the
plastering, the pottery found in the house was typically domestic in
function: bowls, cooking pots, jugs, pitchers, and storage jars. After
the plastering, these domestic forms disappear. Lamps and storage
jars were the only ceramic materials found in this second phase of
the house's use. The artifacts and architecture associated with the
first phase of the building's history clearly mark this building as a
private home. The arch, the new roof, the plastering and the absence
of domestic pottery point conclusively to the conclusion that the
building was no longer a private home but served some sort of a public function. The graffiti makes it quite clear that this public function
was as a Christian house of worship. This house converted into a
church was in use until the middle of the fourth century. In the middle of the fifth century an octagonal church was built directly over it.

Since such octagonal structures usually are built to memorialize some important event of Jesus' life, it is tempting to associate this church with the house of Peter. This is precisely what early pilgrims did to the site, as is clear from the diaries they left.

Fr. Loffreda suggests that the identification of the building below the octagonal church with the house of Peter is "morally" certain. What archaeology has demonstrated is that a private home built in the early Roman period was converted into a place of prayer for Christians in the middle of the first century. In the middle of the fifth century a splendid octagonal church was built on the same spot. Archaeology cannot provide all the answers that we would like. It would be fascinating to know whether the house beneath the octagonal church did in fact provide shelter to Jesus while he stayed in Capernaum. The archaeological evidence is not sufficient to provide a definitive answer. Of course, the first Christian pilgrims who prayed in this house and scratched their confessions of faith upon its walls believed that they were praying in the very room which Jesus called "home" at one period in his life.

Jewish Christianity

In the course of excavating such monumental buildings as the synagogue and octagonal church, small but highly significant finds are made which call for careful study and interpretation. One such find made at Capernaum near the octagonal church was a small (4 × 5 cm) triangular ostracon (a fragment of pottery bearing an inscription). The ostracon dates from the Late Roman to Early Byzantine Period (200–400 A.D.). This range of dates was deduced from the pottery and coins identified from the area in which the ostracon was recovered. Written material like the ostracon is a relatively rare find in excavations which take place in Palestine. The scrolls of Qumran are a happy exception to this rule. Occasionally one can find inscriptions on buildings or graffiti, but these are too infrequent to please the epigrapher and the historian. That is why each inscription found—no matter how fragmentary—is treated as very valuable.

The inscription on the ostracon found at Capernaum is fragmentary. It consists of three lines with a total of nine characters in all. The only way that such an inscription could be read is for the interpreter to supply letters and even entire words which make sense when joined to the few letters which the ostracon bears. Corbo takes the letters to be Hebrew and reconstructs the text to read: "Purify the pitcher of wine, your blood, O Yahweh." On the basis of this reading, Corbo suggests that the ostracon is a fragment of a vessel used for liturgical purposes during the Christian Eucharist. That is quite a conclusion when one remembers that the text being reconstructed contained just nine letters. J. F. Strange in reviewing Corbo's hypothesis offers another reconstruction. He suggests reading the text as Aramaic (which used the same alphabet as Hebrew). He assumes that the inscription was incised on the vessel to indicate ownership, in which case the reconstructed text would have read: "N, the wine-maker; wine which he squeezed. May it be for good." Strange does not maintain that his reading is definitive, but he suggests it merely as an alternative to Corbo's to show that the text can be read without assuming it to be a cultic text.

The great difference between these two reconstructions demonstrates a significant problem in the interpretation of archaeological data. The structures and the artifacts which the archaeologists unearth do not carry identification tags. It is left for the excavators to supply the identification of individual artifacts and then to integrate all data into a coherent interpretation of the site. However, no interpretation takes place within an intellectual vacuum. Every interpreter has a set of presuppositions which serves to guide the process of interpretation and reconstruction. Unfortunately it sometimes happens that an interpreter's presuppositions get in the way of an objective reading of the data. In other words, sometimes archaeologists find what they expect to find. Clearly Corbo resisted this temptation when it came to dating the synagogue but was unable to do so when it came to reconstructing the inscription on the ostracon. Strange was able to read the very same text so differently because he began with the assumption that the text was non-cultic. He acknowledged this assumption and admitted that his reading could not be considered definitive. Corbo did not adequately state the assumptions he had in mind as he began making some sense out of those nine letters scratched on the ostracon.

Corbo and Loffreda had one basic assumption about Capernaum as they began their work. They were guided in their work by the thesis of one of their fellow Franciscans, B. Bagatti, about the existence of "Judaeo-Christians," i.e., Palestinian Jews who accepted Jesus as the Messiah. Bagatti's study of this phenomenon is entitled *The Church from the Circumcision*. It is clear that there were both Christians and Jews present in Capernaum in the fourth century when both the synagogue and the church above the "House of Peter" were in use. Secondly, Talmudic sources speak of *minim* residing at Capernaum. The word *minim* was used by the rabbis to refer to Christians. Despite the work of Bagatti, no clear consensus has been reached about Jewish Christians in Palestine. Raymond Brown suggests that, like other Jews in antiquity, Jews who accepted Jesus as the Messiah displayed a variety of ways to express this faith, and so to speak of Jewish Christianity as if it were a monochromatic phenomenon in antiquity is to simplify what appears to be a complex reality.

Corbo's reconstruction of the partial text on the ostracon found near the octagonal church is based on his assumption of the presence of a Jewish religious community in Capernaum in the fourth to fifth century. That there were Christians and Jews in Capernaum at this time is beyond dispute, but the characterization of the Christian community as "Judaeo-Christian" is going beyond the evidence that is available at the present time. The contours of Jewish Christianity still need clarification before one can postulate the existence of such a group at Capernaum in order to help interpret artifactual data uncovered in the course of excavation.

Conclusion

The excavations at Capernaum are significant not only for what they reveal about the town in antiquity but also because of the important issues of archaeological methodology that they illustrate. The synagogue excavations show how careful stratigraphic excavations can help clarify the history of a structure and guide the reconstruction of the building. Sometimes, as is the case with Capernaum, the results of the excavations will call into question what had been thought of as the "assured results of scholarship." When this happens, a lively debate will certainly ensue, but, in the end, theories, no matter how cherished, will have to give way to tangible evidence.

Secondly, the excavations of the octagonal church point out that careful and controlled digging can provide us with many answers but not always to every question. Is the structure below the octagonal really Peter's house? Excavations have revealed a private house of the Early Roman Period that was converted into a place of worship by Christians sometime in the middle of the first century. This converted structure was in use until the fourth century. In the middle of the fifth century it was covered over by a memorial church. Pilgrims in antiquity who visited this site testified to the belief that they prayed in the house of Peter which was used by Jesus during his stay in Capernaum. However, the archaeologists have not found the kind of evidence that can really confirm this belief. Perhaps they never will. Finally, the reconstruction of a text, a portion of which was found on an ostracon in Capernaum, shows how a theoretical framework always comes into play in the process of interpreting archaeological data. It is clear then that any interpretation offered by archaeologists will be as convincing as is the theoretical framework within which the interpretation is made. Unfortunately the notion of Jewish Christianity has not been clarified to the point that it can be used with confidence in trying to interpret the material remains of Capernaum.

6
Nabratein and Its Ark

Introduction

Until the 1970's, the work of American archaeologists in Palestine was confined almost exclusively to sites connected with the Hebrew Scriptures and the history of ancient Israel. This bias resulted in a neglect of projects which could have helped to illuminate our understanding of Christian origins and the development of early Palestinian Judaism. For the study of these latter two areas there are abundant literary sources, so scholars were willing to be satisfied with these. Yet there was also an abundance of material sources lying beneath the surface of Palestine just waiting for discovery. The reason why New Testament scholars are willing to ignore archaeology is probably related to their almost exclusive concern with the theological dimensions of the Christian Scriptures. Their historical, geographical and sociological dimensions are considered secondary and tangential by many. Perhaps the growing interest in the social milieu out of which the Church emerged will result in more attention to the work of the archaeologist. There has been a similar bias in favor of literary sources among the scholars who study the origins of rabbinic Judaism. This exclusive reliance on texts has led to an over-simplified portrait of early Judaism which is recognized today as a very complex and diverse phenomenon. In the study of both early Christianity and rabbinic Judaism, the use of literary *and* material sources will yield a more comprehensive understanding of the culture which gave rise to these two great faiths.

The growing sensitivity to the importance of non-literary sources has stimulated excavation projects in Galilee, which is a significant region for the study of both early Christianity and Judaism. Jesus and many of his disciples were from Galilee. Many Jews from Jerusalem and its environs fled to Galilee following the two unsuccessful revolts against Rome in A.D. 70 and 135. In the previous chapter we looked at Capernaum which was closely associated with the ministry of Jesus and became a site for Christian pilgrimage to the "House of Peter." In this chapter we will consider the town of Nabratein which can help us understand the world of the early rabbis. While it is correct to say that both towns are located in Galilee, it is important to remember that this region is hardly a single entity. Josephus, the first century Jewish historian and apologist, divided this region into two subdivisions: Upper Galilee and Lower Galilee. Upper Galilee comprises an area of one hundred and eighty square miles dominated by Mount Meiron (approximately four thousand feet above sea level). It extends northward as far as the slopes of the Lebanon range, eastward to the Jordan Valley and west to the area near Acco. Lower Galilee to the south is a much larger area (four hundred and seventy square miles). It extends from Mount Carmel on the west to the Sea of Galilee on the east. Its southern boundary follows a line along the Nazareth fault to Mount Tabor to the southern tip of the Sea of Galilee. Capernaum belongs to lower Galilee while Nabratein belongs to Upper Galilee. Archaeological work in Upper Galilee is a relatively recent phenomenon. Of course, there have been surveys in this region from time to time, but the first full-scale excavations were initiated by E. M. Meyers, J. F. Strange and C. L. Meyers and their Meiron Excavation Project. In a period of ten years, four sites have been studied: Khirbet Shema, Meiron, Gush Halav and Nabratein. The central feature of each of these sites was a synagogue which became the focus of the excavations. It was the ruins of an ancient synagogue which first attracted archaeologists to Nabratein.

The ruins of an ancient town identified as Nabratein are located on a small hill which is four kilometers north of the modern Israeli city of Safed. At present the site is surrounded by a national forest which was planted in 1955. Nabratein is the Arabic name for a town mentioned in the Palestinian Talmud as Neburaya. This source identifies the town as the home of a popular preacher and rabbi named Jacob, who often found himself in conflict with other rabbinic authorities who did not agree with some of his legal decisions. In one source Jacob is denounced as a "sinner," which is understood by some as indicating that he embraced Christianity. Nabratein is also mentioned in a few medieval Jewish texts. The ruins of the ancient settlement were discovered in the late nineteenth century by Charles Wilson and Ernest Renan who noted the presence of an inscribed lintel among the architectural fragments on the site. But apart from a three day period in 1905 when H. Kohl and C. Watzinger sunk some probe trenches and recorded a few architectural fragments, no excavations were attempted at Nabratein though some surveys were made.

The most interesting feature of the ruins noticed in the course of these early surveys of Nabratein was the inscribed limestone lintel. This lintel is a little more than two meters long. In its center is a wreath which encloses a *menorah*. On either side of the wreath is an inscription of some seventy-five letters, most of which are in relief though a few are incised into the limestone. Topping off the lintel is a frieze decorated with laurel leaves. Though the inscription was published as early as 1864, it was not successfully deciphered until amost a century later when N. Avigad translated it in 1960 as follows: "(According) to the number four hundred and ninety-four years after the destruction (of the temple), the house was built during the office of Hanina son of Lezer and Luliana son of Yudan." This inscription follows a formula popular in pagan and Christian inscriptions found in Syria but not the standard form of Palestinian synagogue inscriptions. Here a date is given, and the building of "the house" (synagogue) under the leadership of certain officials is commemorated.

The date on the lintel is equivalent to A.D. 564—a date which is somewhat problematic on both historical and architectural grounds. First of all, the imperial policy in the Byzantine Period severely restricted the freedom of Jews. In 545 Emperor Justinian reconfirmed earlier laws which forbade the building of any new synagogues. In addition the day witnessed forced conversions of Jews to Christianity, the desecration of synagogues and other outrages. These policies of the Byzantine emperors were responsible for the growth of animosity between Christians and Jews in Palestine, and occasionally this animosity spilled over into violence, as it did in 556 when Jews and Samaritans rioted against the government in Caesarea. In the wake of these tensions and events, it is highly unlikely that the people of Nabratein would have been able to erect a synagogue in 564. Secondly, the remaining architectural fragments found along with the lintel as well as the lintel itself reflect the style of the Late Roman Period (150–350). Finally, excavations at three nearby sites (Gush Halav, Meiron and Khirbet Shema) indicate that these sites ceased to exist by the sixth century, but apparently Nabratein was still flourishing. Avigad suggested that the lintel was part of a Late Roman building which was being renovated in the sixth century. The inscription simply commemorates this renovation rather than the construction of the synagogue. Clearly one objective of any excavation project at Nabratein would be to clarify the history of the synagogue and explain the anomaly of the sixth century date found on what appeared to be a lintel from at least two hundred years earlier.

The Synagogue

Excavations at Nabratein proceeded quite quickly and were completed in just two seasons. At the end of this period, one major objective was met: the history of the synagogue became clear. The strategy of the excavation project was to focus attention on the synagogue and the area immediately surrounding it. This is where most of the effort was expended. Of course, areas outside the synagogue were excavated in order to sample the domestic occupation of the village and to describe the demographic context in which the synagogue was located. A few meters northeast of the synagogue the area was disturbed by a modern lime kiln. Modern entrepreneurs dug out a kiln in order to process lime to be used as fertilizer. They chose this spot since the synagogue's ruins provided a ready supply of limestone for their kiln. Many of the architectural fragments recorded by Kohl and Watzinger were not located in the course of this project. No doubt they were consumed in the kiln. Fortunately the two German archaeologists provided us with a record of the now lost architectural fragments. The kiln did serve some practical use since it became the project's dump.

The first season of work on the synagogue confirmed Avigad's theory of a Byzantine period renovation of the synagogue which was originally constructed much earlier. The issue which still remained in doubt was the date of the original founding of the building. The Middle Roman Period (70–150) pottery found beneath the earliest floor indicated that the first structure on the site was erected prior to the Late Roman Period (150–350). The second season of work settled the question. The first structure was in fact founded in the Middle Roman Period. It was a broadhouse synagogue whose external dimensions were 11.6 × 9.3 meters. Its roof was probably supported by two rows of columns, though excavation did not reveal their exact location. The floor of this first rather simple building was plastered. On either side of the main door to the synagogue which was located in the southern wall (the wall of orientation), there were two stone platforms. One of these was probably the synagogue's *bema* (a podium from which the Scripture was read during the service); the other probably served to support the Holy Ark in which the sacred scrolls were kept.

This first synagogue served the needs of the village for over one hundred years. During that time, Nabratein's population grew to such an extent that by the middle of the third century a larger building for worship was needed. Rather than constructing an entirely new building on a different site, the people of Nabratein simply enlarged their Middle Roman synagogue. An extension was added onto the northern end of the building so that the new structure now measured 11.6 × 13.75 meters. The interior architecture of the building changed as a result, for the synagogue was no longer a broadhouse but it became a basilica with two rows of three columns each. The entranceway was enlarged and beautified. The lintel (without the later inscription) dates from this renovation. The beautiful lintel with its menorah surrounded by a wreath was not the only decorative element which adorned this synagogue. Excavations unearthed evidence of a surprising amount of animal sculptures at Nabratein. Evidently the villagers at Nabratein did not interpret the biblical prohibition of images (Ex 20:4, Dt 5:8) to include all representational art. The lions, eagles, rabbits and other animal figures which decorated this synagogue are a striking exception to the general pattern found elsewhere in the synagogues of Upper Galilee. These were generally devoid of the kind of representational art which the people of Nabratein found quite acceptable. These animal sculptures and other decorative elements which adorned the Late Roman Period synagogue are fine examples of skilled craftmanship of the stone masons who plied their trade in this period.

An earthquake struck the region in 306 and the synagogue gives evidence of having been damaged by the tremor. This is clear from the reconstruction work that took place in the early part of the fourth century. While the building did not collapse, various elements did sustain serious damage. The reconstruction project consisted in laying a new floor, strengthening of the platform on which the columns rested, and the reconstruction of the two platforms that flank the main entrance of the building. The renovations were completed rather quickly, and the building once again served the village—this time for more than fifty years. In 363 another earthquake struck the region, but this time repairs were not made on the building since the village was dying. In fact, the entire region of Upper Galilee was suffering from some problem which resulted in one village after another being abandoned. Nabratein was abandoned for some two hundred years. What precipitated this situation is not clear. In 351 there was a revolt against Roman rule in Palestine, but it is doubtful whether the effects of this unsuccessful revolt reached the relatively isolated villages of Upper Galilee. A more probable cause for the wane of Nabratein and some of its neighboring villages was the excessive taxation during the reign of Constantius II (mid-fourth century). The economic hardships caused by the taxation caused the population of Upper Galilee to disperse. Many came to settle in the Golan which was directly east. Whatever the reason for the abandonment of Nabratein, the village was not resettled until the middle of the sixth century.

Once the town was resettled in the Byzantine period, work started on the reconstruction of the synagogue which was in ruins since the mid-fourth century. If Avigad's reading of the inscription on the lintel is correct, the synagogue was rededicated in 564. The resettlement of the village was no half-hearted affair since the synagogue had to be expanded for a second time. Again the expansion meant movement of the north wall, so that the dimensions of the Byzantine synagogue were 16.9 × 11.6 meters. The interior architecture remained basilical but now with two rows of *four* columns each. In addition, there were two rows of benches along its interior walls, though only a small remnant of these survived until the present. The entrance to the building was from the south through a single wide door beneath the inscribed lintel. This required the worshipers to make a 180° turn after entering in order to orient themselves for the service which was to be conducted with the participants facing Jerusalem to the south. The necessity for such a maneuver is clear from the presence of a *bema* on each side of the entrance way. The floor was made up of flagstone pavers founded on cobbles laid into plaster. A gold coin of Justinian I was found immediately below the threshold of the doorway. It was probably placed there deliberately in connection with the reconstruction work, and it confirms Avigad's reading of the inscription on the lintel, since Justinian was emperor in 564.

There were then four phases of the synagogue's history. The first building was a broadhouse erected in the early second century. Around 250 the building was expanded into a basilica and was in use until 306 when it was damaged by an earthquake. After a rapid rebuild the synagogue remained in use until another earthquake which struck in 363. No reconstruction of the building was attempted, since the economic misfortunes of Upper Galilee meant that Nabratein was losing its population to the Golan. In the middle of the sixth century a sizable Jewish population returned to Nabratein. The synagogue was not only rebuilt but enlarged. The village was again abandoned in the latter half of the seventh century during the Islamic invasion.

The Ark

In the course of work on the synagogue, the excavators came up with a genuinely unique find. It was a find which an overly romanticized image of archaeology considers commonplace, but which experienced archaeologists know to be rare indeed. During the last few days of work in the second and final season of excavation, it was decided to dismantle the western *bema* of the second Late Roman synagogue. Though this procedure was not really necessary for the clarification of the synagogue's history, additional support for the conclusions about the synagogue would have been welcome. Work started on dislodging a large limestone building block from the top layer of the *bema*. The only equipment available to facilitate this effort was a tripod outfitted with block and tackle. After careful preparations to forestall any danger to the workers and to the stone itself, the large stone was gradually extricated from the place where it lay undisturbed for nearly seventeen hundred years. As the stone emerged from its ancient setting, it became clear that this was no ordinary limestone building block. As the stone's underside became visible, its function in the ancient synagogue also became clear. The synagogue of Nabratein had yielded its holy ark—its Torah shrine. The stone which had been patiently culled from the *bema* was the pediment of a Torah shrine which served as the shelter for the sacred scrolls that were read during the synagogue's religious services. In its original state, the pediment would have rested on two pillars, but these were not found.

The pediment was decorated with an embossed rosette which was located just below its peaked roof. Along the roof line there were egg and dart moldings. The center of the pediment was decorated with a scallop-shell carving. There was a hole notched into the shell, presumably for the chain which supported an oil lamp whose light was to burn perpetually before the ark. Finally on each side of the roof there was a rampant lion executed quite beautifully in the lime-

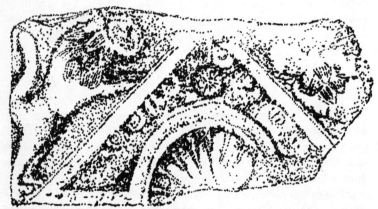

A pediment stone, with shell motif and rampant lions, from the Holy Ark of the Synagogue of Nabratein.

stone. All these decorative features were common in Jewish and Roman art of the period. They represented motifs of fertility and
immortality. The pediment and its decorative features make it quite
clear that the ark was the central element of the synagogue's appointments. This, in turn, underscored the importance of the reading of
Scripture within the liturgy of the synagogue. What made this find so
significant was that it was the first such find from antiquity. The earliest example of a Torah shrine found previous to the one from Nabratein dated from the Middle Ages. Of course, there were
depictions of such shrines on coins, glass, pottery, sarcophagi and
friezes but the pediment found at Nabratein is the first fragment of
an actual Torah shrine found in the Holy Land. Presumably most of
these shrines were made of wood which could not have survived to
the present. Nabratein's ark was skillfully carved from limestone
which withstood the vagaries of time very well.

The question which immediately posed itself was: How did the
pediment of the Nabratein ark come to be placed *in* the western
bema of the rebuild phase of the Late Roman synagogue? Obviously
this was a secondary usage; originally the ark would have stood *on*
the *bema*. The ark was probably damaged during the earthquake of
306 to such an extent that it could not be restored to its original position within the synagogue. Yet the sacredness of the ark did not permit the shattered fragment to be thrown out like so much debris. In
the course of reconstructing the earthquake-damaged synagogue, the
people of Nabratein had a brilliant idea: Why not use the remaining
fragment of the ark to rebuild the *bema?* In effect, the pediment was
"buried" within the *bema* where it remained until the summer of
1981. The likely scenario helped to clear up a puzzle from the previous year's work. Excavation under the flooring of the Late Roman
synagogue revealed a pit which contained hundreds of broken roof
tiles. Why these relatively inexpensive ceramic tiles were "buried" in
a pit which seemed to be hewn for that very purpose was not clear
until the pediment was found. Evidently these roof tiles were also
part of the ark, and so, though they too were damaged by the earthquake, they could not be treated as trash. After all, these tiles and the
pediment once sheltered the holy scrolls and so they partook of the
holiness of the Scriptures themselves. They were reverently hidden
away in a corner of the synagogue near the place where the original

ark once stood. All this is evidence of the great importance the Scriptures had for early Judaism. Even the structures which housed the scrolls partook of the holiness of the Scriptures themselves and had to be treated accordingly, even when they could no longer serve their original purpose.

The pediment measures 1.3 meters long, 0.58 meters high and 0.50 meters thick. The original dimensions of the fragment before the damage inflicted by the earthquake would have been somewhat larger. The top, front end of the pediment is severely battered. The top of the gable is broken off as are the lions' heads. Approximately one-third of the stone's right side is missing. The kind of damage which was inflicted on the stone is congruent with that which would result from the effects of an earthquake. Despite the heavy damage, more than enough of the pediment remains to give testimony to the artistry of its ancient sculptors and to support the identification of the stone as a pediment of a Torah shrine. This identification was made primarily on the basis of similarities between the Nabratein fragment and depictions of Torah shrines found in early Jewish art in Israel and the diaspora.

The significance of this find cannot be underestimated. It is now quite obvious that the Jews of third century Galilee held the Scriptures in the highest esteem. The obvious resemblance of the ark to the temple suggests that the ark of the synagogue was viewed as the spiritual successor of the biblical ark of the covenant which was the symbol of the divine presence within the temple. The structure which housed the Scriptures came to be seen in a similar light. That is why the villagers of Nabratein thought it unseemly to just discard the damaged pediment and its broken roof tiles when they were beyond repair. Secondly the decorative motifs of the pediment showed that the villagers were as much at home in the Roman world as they were in the world of their ancient Israelite ancestors. The decorative motifs which adorned the Nabratein ark were fully reflective of the artistic style of the contemporary Roman world. The rampant lions showed that the people of Nabratein felt no hesitation about the use of representational art even in connection with this most sacred object.

The holy ark of the synagogue came to serve the same function as did the temple which had been destroyed for almost two hundred years when the villagers of Nabratein erected their first simple broadhouse synagogue. The synagogue became the place where the divine might be encountered through prayerful reading of the Scriptures. The ark of Nabratein is a powerful reminder of the human quest for the divine which it and its synagogue represent. Archaeology, like no other discipline, can provide us with such tangible and beautiful proofs of how seriously our ancestors took their life with God.

7
The Future of Biblical Archaeology

There have been a number of recent developments in the field of archaeology as it is practiced in the Near East. These developments will dictate the future directions of what has been known as biblical archaeology. It was not very long ago that it was possible for a group of biblical scholars with a minimum of field experience to go to Palestine, receive a permit to excavate and begin a project financed fully by their schools. While these excavation projects met the standards of their day, today they are considered amateurish and even primitive. Today's archaeologists face a knowledge-explosion in their field which requires a certain amount of specialization if they expect to keep current with developments within the discipline. It is an understatement to say that at the present moment biblical archaeology is entering a period of significant change.

The first of these developments is somewhat extraneous to the field of archaeology itself but does have a profound effect on its future. Excavation projects have become very expensive. Field archaeologists today consider the price tag of $200,000 per year as a real bargain in maintaining a project in the field and in supporting a permanent staff to be responsible for publication. This cost reflects the growing sophistication of archaeological methods both in the field and in the laboratory. As these costs rise, it will become more and more difficult for theological schools and small colleges to support excavation projects. In fact, these costs are too high for even large universities to bear alone. Some financial aid has been forthcoming from governmental agencies, but the budget-cutting going on in federal government makes this support questionable for the future. Some private foundations have begun to offer some help. With the advent of governmental and private financing for archaeological projects, there comes some measure of control—even if in an indirect way. For example, proposals for grants have to be written in such a way as to present the goals of the project as advancing humanistic learning rather than some specific religious aims. To survive financially biblical archaeology may need to become a "secular" discipline which has to compete with other scholarly disciplines for the few available dollars to support its research projects.

A second development is the emergence of the Israeli "school" of archaeology. Before the establishment of the state of Israel in 1948, there were a number of national "schools" of archaeology in Palestine. Each had its own projects. For example, the American Schools of Oriental Research has been working in Palestine since 1900. It has sponsored scores of excavations. The British School of Archaeology in Jerusalem was founded in 1919. Its most prominent archaeologist was Kathleen Kenyon whose work at Jericho in the 1950's was a model for its methodological innovations. The German school was established in 1902 and was directed by such notables as Albrecht Alt and Martin Noth. The French School dates to 1892 and is most renowned for the excavation of Qumran under the direction of Roland deVaux, O.P. In the last thirty years Israelis have been taking their rightful place in directing archaeological projects within their borders. Among some of the more important sites excavated by Israeli teams are Hazor, Masada, Beersheba, Dan and Jerusalem. The universities of Israel have important, well staffed and professionally equipped archaeological institutes. Each year these universities graduate a number of archaeologists trained on the doctoral level. These graduates have extensive field and laboratory experience and are prepared to lead their own projects. The logistical, financial and personnel problems facing an Israeli excavation team are small compared to those of foreign teams. This leads one to speculate how long foreigners can compete with Israelis for the ever fewer excavation permits that will be available in the future. Most likely Israelis will themselves take responsibility for most of the projects in their own country. Dependence on foreign schools is an anachronism.

Some may lament this situation and say that this trend effectively transforms biblical archaeology into an "armchair" pursuit for all but the Israelis. Yet this is exactly how G. Ernest Wright, himself a leading archaeologist and *the* teacher of American field archaeologists, envisioned biblical archaeology. In one of his few theoretical works on the subject, Wright defined biblical archaeology as "a special 'armchair' variety of general archaeology, which studies the discoveries of excavators and gleans from them every fact that throws direct, indirect or even diffused light upon the Bible." Wright went on to say that while biblical archaeology must be concerned with methodological issues, its absorbing interest is the understanding and exposition of the Scriptures. Such an aim is not a vital concern for Israeli archaeologists. They are secular scholars who are not connected with the biblical departments of their universities. They read the Bible as a document of their national history rather than as a confessional statement. They are engaged in their archaeological projects in order to understand their ancestors' culture and history—not to illuminate the theological meaning of the Bible. While these aims of the Israeli archaeologists are certainly legitimate, there remain other legitimate concerns. Among these is the attempt to relate the finds of excavations to the area of biblical studies. It is the latter concern that will occupy the study and research of the biblical archaeologists of the future while the actual field work will be in the hands of others.

A third development is the beginning of serious communication with archaeologists who work outside the Near East—notably the "New World" archaeologists. The latter show a greater concern for the broader cultural and anthropological issues than have archaeologists who have worked only in Palestine. New World archaeologists usually find themselves excavating sites inhabited by people who have left no written records. The only "text" these excavators have in hand are ethnographic studies of living primitive societies which can be useful in interpreting some of the material remains of long extinct groups. The objective of New World archaeology is also much more comprehensive than that of biblical archeology. It is nothing less than a clarification of the cultural process—why cultures are diverse and how they change. On the other hand, biblical archaeology has focused almost exclusively on political history, i.e., on the chronology of political events at the site being excavated. This is evident from the strategy of excavation at biblical sites. Archaeologists are eager to find "destruction layers" which are certainly basic to establishing the stratigraphy of a site. But such eagerness myopically misfocuses the excavator's eyes on the catastrophic events of public life and away from the normal everyday life of ordinary people. Similarly excavators are drawn to monumental structures and fortifications. The homes and streets of the common folk are secondary concerns. Finally biblical archaeologists are obsessed with establishing the ceramic chronology of their sites. The emphasis is on the *chronology*. Since archaeologists will generally find what they are looking for, biblical archaeologists will leave the field with an outline of their site's political history and their ceramic sequence. Unfortunately they have often overlooked the larger issues of culture and society. Biblical archaeology's attention has been too narrowly fixed on history.

Serious interchange with New World archaeologists will open biblical archaeologists to theoretical developments in the wider field of archaeology. This will permit them to learn more from their sites than simple political history. Such an interchange will help biblical archaeologists see the nature and significance of artifacts in cultural terms rather than in strictly historical terms. In other words, biblical archaeology will be moved more toward *explanation* instead of being satisfied with *description*. New World archaeologists are accustomed to facing questions largely ignored by their colleagues who work in the Near East. The former try to account for the process of social change. They are not satisfied with simply documenting that change took place at one point in a given society's history. The ultimate aim of archaeology should be the fuller appreciation of human nature, thought and action. To aim for anything less is to be satisfied with a less than adequate use of the data. In the past biblical archaeology was not interested in these anthropological issues since it was simply an adjunct of biblical studies. Its principal value was as an aid in the interpretation of the Scriptures.

The somewhat broader, humanistic goals of New World archaeology were not fully appreciated in the past because of what can be described as the narrow and parochial interest of biblical archaeologists in political history. As long as archaeology was used to clarify the "historical" narratives of the Bible, these larger issues seemed irrelevant. For example, what value is there in hydrological and geological analysis of the water and soil of Jericho if one is simply looking for evidence of a destruction level in the stratum of the Late Bronze Age in order to support the narrative of Joshua 6? New World archaeologists consider such analysis basic to understanding the sites they excavate. How else can one understand how the ancients used their environment for agricultural purposes? In the past, biblical archaeologists considered such issues peripheral. This is no longer the case—due primarily to increased communication with the discipline of general archaeology.

This new interest in broader anthropological issues does not mean that the archaeology of biblical sites will lose its interest in history. The wider humanistic thrust of New World archaeology can be successfully and productively combined with the traditional historical concerns of biblical archaeology. Historically oriented projects such as those that are undertaken in the Near East can be situated within a wider anthropological context if biblical archaeologists will be prepared to ask more questions as they excavate—if they are willing to be sensitive to all the information which their excavation yields. Similarly such a concern will help provide a needed corrective to some biblical archaeologists who assume that the archaeological record can be converted directly into historical facts. This new approach to the excavation of biblical sites not only will help us understand the progress of historical events but will also aid us in our attempt to understand the lives of very ordinary people. Clarification of the cultural process is really an attempt at self-understanding. Certainly one of the goals of the Bible is to aid the self-understanding of its readers. In pursuing these humanistic, anthropological goals, biblical archaeology will help the Bible's message be understood as much as it ever did.

All of the foregoing bespeaks the need for a more professional approach to the archaeological enterprise in the Near East. It is no longer realistic to expect that it is possible or even desirable for excavation projects to be carried on by "part-timers" whose real work is biblical interpretation. In the past archaeology was at best a summertime avocation for biblical scholars whose principal responsibility was teaching in theological seminaries. While such people did achieve an admirable level of competency, improved standards and techniques in the field of archaeology call for full-time professional archaeologists whose area of teaching and research is in the discipline of archaeology exclusively. A corollary of this expectation is that the archaeologists of the future should receive the kind of training that will prepare them for full-time work in their field. The first generation of biblical archaeologists were usually trained in biblical studies. Some did have an opportunity for supplementary field work at some excavation. The next generation of archaeologists will have to receive a much broader, multi-disciplinary preparation, including the study of anthropology, ethnology, geology, botany, zoology, statistics and computer technology. Since biblical archaeology is broadening its horizons and is developing new methods of field work and interpretation, its practitioners will have to receive appropriate preparation. This concern for professionalism is then a response to the changes in the way archaeological projects proceed today. The results of this concern will be greater achievements in the field and more trustworthy interpretation of recovered data. At the very least, it may improve the dismal record of publication. The fact that a precious few of the American excavation projects in Israel instituted since 1950 have produced final and comprehensive reports is due in some measure to the part-time status of those who have directed these projects. Such a situation ought not to continue and is itself an argument for an increased sense of professionalism among biblical archaeologists.

The final trend that calls for our attention is the proposal that the term "biblical archaeology" be abandoned. Although such a suggestion has been made by a number of archaeologists, its most vocal proponent is William Dever, one of the excavators of Gezer. He has suggested in a number of publications that the term biblical archaeology be replaced by "Syro-Palestinian" archaeology. While some of Dever's colleagues dismiss this suggestion as just a matter of semantics, Dever is quite serious about this substitution, for he sees this change in nomenclature as reflective of what ought to be happening in the archaeological projects underway in the Near East. In Dever's view there is a revolution going on in the field of archaeology which he applauds. He sees the growing concern for professionalism in archaeology as freeing this discipline from what he calls "the domination of biblical studies." Once this happens archaeology can achieve its own identity and pursue its own goals as an academic discipline in its own right rather than as an adjunct to biblical studies. Dever maintains that the term "biblical archaeology" sows the seeds of confusion by intimating that there is a brand of archaeology whose function it is to confirm the Bible and that the value of the Bible is enhanced by such confirmation. The term "Syro-Palestinian archaeology" will carry no such theological freight.

Dever defines Syro-Palestinian archaeology as that branch of general archaeology which deals with the geographical, cultural and chronological entity which embraced the distinctive land bridge between Egypt and Mesopotamia with a succession of cultures from 3500 B.C. to the Greco-Roman and Byzantine periods. By this definition Syro-Palestinian archaeology extends far beyond the time period and subject matter of the Bible. The name itself is derived from the ancient name for what is now Syria, Lebanon, Jordan and Israel. Palestine in most periods of antiquity was merely a subprovince of Syria and cannot be discussed independently of it. For Dever, then, Syro-Palestinian archaeology is a secular discipline whose goals, assumptions and methods are determined by archaeology and not by the special concerns of biblical scholarship. Dever admits that there may be some who are not interested in the entire broad sweep of the discipline as he defines it. Those interested in the periods which produced the Bible ought to use the term "archaeology of the biblical period" which Dever considers a legitimate specialization within the general field of Syro-Palestinian archaeology.

This suggestion reinforces what should be obvious: the Bible, like all literary sources, is a secondary source for archaeologists. The primary data are the artifacts which are uncovered in the process of excavation. The remains of the material culture—the houses, temples, fortifications, coins, lithic and metallic objects, bones—are the raw materials of archaeology. These are its primary data. While the Bible can be used to clarify some of the data, it has little or no relevance for some periods which are studied by Syro-Palestinian archaeology. The goal of this discipline then is not the clarification of the Bible but the recovery of the material culture of antiquity which is studied in order to have some idea of the thoughts, beliefs and behavior of ancient societies. The means used to attain that goal include every modern archaeological technique to wring the maximum information from the earth whether or not that information has any immediate bearing on the Bible. Dever sees these efforts as pure science, i.e., research done for its own sake without any attempt to justify its existence by calling it "biblical archaeology."

In addition to these theoretical considerations, Dever sees some very practical consequences to this change in nomenclature. First of all, it will free archaeology and biblical studies to proceed independently of one another according to the principles and methods proper to each discipline with uncompromised integrity. Secondly, it will allow archaeology to develop its full potential by freeing it from the very narrow concern for political history which limited the field for too long. Finally, the practitioners of Syro-Palestinian archaeology will be full-time archaeologists with the freedom and resources that come with that status. This should allow them to go about their tasks—especially when it comes to publication—with a new level of sophistication and productivity.

Understandably Dever's suggestions have raised a storm of protest from his colleagues who are content and even proud of the self-designation "biblical archaeologist." They reject Dever's argument that the term "biblical archaeology" smacks of fundamentalism as if legitimate biblical archaeologists are people who seek to "prove" the Bible is true by mounting expeditions to find Noah's ark. While there are people who attempt just that and other quixotic projects such as looking for Moses' grave, the garden of Eden and the ark of the covenant, these people are not really archaeologists at all. Biblical archaeology is an empirical study, a critical discipline that proceeds according to accepted scholarly standards. It is a sub-specialty of biblical studies which attempts to make use of all information gained through archaeological research and study in order to facilitate the interpretation of the Bible. In other words, biblical archaeology attempts to answer questions about the societies which produced the Bible. Dever's critics, who include H. Darrell Lance, his colleague from the Gezer excavations, suggest that Dever's professionalism is often just a cloak for esotericism. They bristle at the suggestion that their projects were just amateurish even though Dever was quick to point out that amateurs are not necessarily incompetent. They find nothing wrong about making the elucidation of the biblical text as a main concern for their archaeological projects. Their hope is that biblical scholars and archaeologists will work more closely together in order to bring archaeological data more to bear on biblical studies. They fear that Dever will drive a wedge between archaeology and biblical studies.

Too often archaeological data are simply ignored by biblical scholars. Commentaries are published which do not even allude to the archaeological data revelant to a particular text. For example, one of the most important commentaries on the Books of Kings is the one by John Gray in the Old Testament Library series, yet it does not contain a single archaeological illustration, photograph or drawing even though the Books of Kings lend themselves quite readily to the inclusion of archaeological material. In happy contrast stand Robert Boling's commentaries on Joshua and Judges in the Anchor Bible series. Both of these commentaries give careful consideration to the way archaeology can help shed light on some of the perplexing difficulties in the interpretation of the biblical text. If Syro-Palestinian archaeology goes its own way and becomes totally absorbed in alluvial deposits and pollen analysis, it will become easier for biblical scholars to ignore archaeology, and what is a neglected source now will become entirely lost. It may be necessary to have paleoethnobiologists and geologists on an excavation staff as Dever suggests. Why should there not be on the very same staff someone whose sole responsibility is to relate the findings of the dig to biblical scholars so that they may use this data in their own research? Something must be done to help exegetes assimilate the results of excavation projects in order to incorporate them in their study of the Bible.

The debate regarding Dever's suggestion will go on for some time because it makes legitimate and necessary points regarding the need for more professionalism in archaeological projects and for more attention to theoretical developments in the discipline outside the Near East. But it will not be easy to abandon the term "biblical archaeology." It does have a strong tradition standing behind it in American biblical scholarship of the Albright and Wright school. In addition an archaeological approach is one of the several valid ways to study the Bible. Dever is correct, however, when he points out that in the popular mind archaeology has a fundamentalist tinge. It does smack of "proving" the Bible to be true no matter what archaeologists say. In fact, even on the critical level there have been attempts to use archaeological data to demonstrate that the biblical narratives about the patriarchs (Gen 12–50) reflect the conditions of a so-called patriarchal age (late second millennium B.C.). There have also been attempts to demonstrate that the Book of Joshua is an accurate representation of the manner in which the Israelite tribes acquired their land in Canaan. The real agenda behind both of these attempts was less a concern to show how the Bible can be better understood through archaeology than to demonstrate the historicity of biblical narratives. The need to demonstrate the latter derives not from archaeology but from a certain theological bent. Dever is correct when he says that the scope of biblical archaeology as practiced by Americans has been too narrowly focused on the historical reconstruction of the Israelite period. The New Testament period was ignored because it required no such historical reconstruction and in any case its message was primarily theological. Christian and rabbinic sites have been ignored up to now for the most part since they do not shed any direct light on the Bible. With such a prevailing attitude, it is no wonder that some projects overlook strata from the Islamic period in order to get to the "really important" Israelite strata. Dever's suggestions will make the archaeologists working the Near East careful to extricate every bit of evidence from their sites. Finally Dever's concerns about the training of future archaeologists and the funding of projects must be attended to as biblical archaeologists chart the future of their discipline.

Biblical archaeology has come a long way from the days of Edward Robinson's journeys through Palestine on the back of a donkey in 1838. William Flinders Petrie changed the course of archaeological technique in 1890 when he developed a system of identifying the strata of a site on the basis of their contents, particularly the pottery. Between the World Wars various national schools of archaeology operating in Palestine sponsored numerous projects and developed the methods of excavation to such an extent that archaeology was on the road to becoming a genuine scholarly enterprise rather than the West's plundering of the East's cultural heritage. Another revolution took place when the Wheeler method of stratigraphic excavation was adapted to the Palestinian situation by Kathleen Kenyon in the 1950's. This new method introduced "control" into the process of excavation through careful digging and meticulous recording. It was this element of control that made archaeology a genuine science. The revolution that is now going on in biblical archaeology is the attempt to expand the horizons of the discipline through conversation with archaeologists who work outside the Near East. This has led to the use of new techniques of excavation and new procedures in the interpretation of data with the result that biblical archaeology is moving beyond the description of the material remains of an ancient site to the interpretation and understanding of the cultural process itself.

Biblical archaeology is entering a period of significant change. That is all for the good, since it shows that the discipline is still alive and its practitioners are engaging in the kind of creative self-criticism that leads to new vigorous growth in integrity, scholarship and productivity. Interest in this discipline will always be keen as long as there is interest in the Bible. Our fascination with archaeology is just one way we have learned to express our fascination with the Bible.

Bibliography

Chapter 1

The relationship of archaeology to the Bible has always been somewhat problematic. The following works by important biblical archaeologists describe some of the different ways they have tried to relate the results of their field work with the Bible.

Albright, William F., *The Archaeology of Palestine*. Baltimore: Penguin Books, 1960.

Freedman, David N., *New Directions in Biblical Archaeology*. Garden City, N.Y.: Doubleday, 1969.

Kenyon, Kathleen M., *Archaeology in the Holy Land*. London: Benn, 1979.

Paul, Shalom M. and Dever, William G., eds., *Biblical Archaeology*. Jerusalem: Keter, 1974.

Sanders, James A., *Near Eastern Archaeology in the Twentieth Century*. Garden City, N.Y.: Doubleday, 1970.

Wright, G. Ernest, *Biblical Archaeology*. Philadelphia: Westminster, 1962.

On Kuntillet Ajrud

Meshel, Zeev, *Kuntillet Ajrud*. Jerusalem: Israeli Museum, 1978.

———, "Did Yahweh Have a Consort? The New Religious Inscriptions from Sinai," *Biblical Archaeology Review* 5 (March/April 1979) 24–35.

Chapter 2

Ben-Tor, A., "The Regional Study: A New Approach to Archaeological Investigation," *Biblical Archaeology Review* 6 (1980) 30–44. A good illustration of how a regional study works and the guidance it provides to field archaeologists in planning their work.

Dever, W.G., "Archaeological Method in Israel: A Continuing Revolution," *Biblical Archeologist* 43 (1980) 41–48. A brief historical review of critical moments in the development of archaeological methods from the nineteenth century to the present with a projection of archaeology's future.

Dever, W.G. and Lance, H.D., eds., *A Manual of Field Excavation: Handbook for Field Archaeologists.* New York: Hebrew Union College, 1978. A guide to the principles and methods of field archaeology based on the Wheeler-Kenyon method. Well illustrated.

Kenyon, K., *Beginning in Archaeology.* 3rd revised edition. New York: F.A. Praeger, 1972. An excellent presentation of the stratigraphic approach to excavation; it focuses on archaeology in Palestine.

Lance, H.D., *The Old Testament and the Archaeologist.* Philadelphia: Fortress, 1981. A popularly written introduction to archaeological method with a focus on the Solomonic Age (tenth century B.C.).

Meyers, E.W. and Strange, J.F., "Survey in Galilee: 1976," *Explor* 3 (1977) 7–17. Another example of a regional study.

Wheeler, M., *Archaeology from the Earth.* Oxford: Clarendon Press, 1955. The classic text on the stratigraphic approach to field archaeology.

Chapter 3

Archi, A., "The Epigraphic Evidence from Ebla and the Old Testament," *Biblica* 60 (1979), pp. 556–566.

———, "Further Concerning Ebla and the Bible," *Biblical Archeologist* 44 (1981), pp. 145–154.

Very polemical refutations of Pettinato's readings of some Ebla texts by the man who replaced him as the epigrapher of the Mardikh expedition.

Bermant, C. and Weitzman, M., *Ebla: A Revelation in Archaeology.* New York: Times Books, 1979. A balanced account of the Ebla finds free from the polemics that surface in most other presentations. Highly recommended because it provides reliable information that is tailored to the general reader.

Dahood, M., "Are the Ebla Tablets Relevant to Biblical Research?" *Biblical Archaeology Review* 6 (1980), pp. 54–59.

———, "Ebla, Ugarit and the Old Testament," *Vetus Testamentum*, Supplement 29 (1978), pp. 81–112.

The author attempts to show how obscure passages from the Bible may be clarified on the basis of words from the Ebla tablets; his method and conclusions remain controversial.

Gelb, I.J., *Thoughts about Ebla.* Syro-Mesopotamian Studies I. 1977. A short monograph evaluating some early historical, cultural and linguistic data from Ebla by a leading Semitist; a useful corrective to some of Pettinato's earlier readings.

Matthiae, P., *Ebla: An Empire Rediscovered.* Garden City, N.Y.: Doubleday, 1980. A discussion of the archaeological evidence from Ebla written in such a way that a good portion of the book will be of interest to specialists; makes only four references to Pettinato.

Pettinato, G., *The Archives of Ebla.* Garden City, N.Y.: Doubleday, 1981. A study of Ebla's culture based on the author's reading of some one hundred and sixty tablets; intended for the general reader but much is directed at the author's colleagues; contains a seventy-page "afterword" by Dahood on Ebla and the Bible.

Chapter 4

Accounts and Criticism of Early Works on the Ophel

Kenyon, Kathleen, M., *The Bible and Recent Archaeology.* Atlanta: Knox, 1978, pp. 44–66.

———, *Digging up Jerusalem.* London: Benn, 1976, 288 pp.

———, *Royal Cities of the Old Testament.* New York: Schocken, 1971, pp. 13–52.

Stager, Lawrence E., "The Archaeology of the Eastern Slope of Jerusalem and the Terraces of the Kidron," *Journal of Near Eastern Studies* 41 (1982) 111–121.

Shiloh's Preliminary Reports

Shiloh, Yigal, "City of David Excavation 1978," *Biblical Archeologist* 42 (1979) 165–171.

———, "The City of David Archaeological Project: The Third Season— 1980," *Biblical Archeologist* 44 (1981) 161–170.

Popular Accounts of the Ophel Project

Hamblin, Dora Jane, "Bearing Witness to the City of David's Life and Death," *Smithsonian* 13 (July 1982) 73–83.

Shiloh, Yigal, "The Rediscovery of Warren's Shaft," *Biblical Archaeology Review* 7 (July/August 1981) 24–39.

—— and Kaplan, Mendel, "Digging in the City of David," *Biblical Archaeology Review* 5 (July/August 1979) 36–49.

Controversies Surrounding the Ophel Project

Shanks, Hershel, "New York Times Misrepresents Major Jerusalem Discovery," *Biblical Archaeology Review* 7 (July/August 1981) 40–43.

——, "Politics at the City of David," *Biblical Archaeology Review* 7 (November/December 1981) 40–44.

Chapter 5

General Introductions to the Archaeological Finds at Capernaum

Avi-Yonah, M., "Capernaum," in the *Encyclopedia of Archaeological Excavations in the Holy Land.* Englewood Cliffs, N.J.: Prentice-Hall, 1975, Vol. 1, pp. 286–290.

Loffreda, S., *A Visit to Capernaum.* 2nd ed. Jerusalem: Franciscan Printing Press, 1973.

Strange, J.F., "Capernaum" *Interpreter's Dictionary of the Bible.* Supplement, pp. 140–141.

Additional Information About the Synagogue

Avi-Yonah, M., "Ancient Synagogues," *Ariel* 32 (1973) 29–43.

——, "Editor's Note," *Israel Exploration Journal* 23 (1973) 43–45.

Chiat, M.J.S., *Handbook of Synagogue Architecture.* Chico, Calif.: Scholars Press, 1982, pp. 89–97.

Foerster, G., "Notes on Recent Excavations at Capernaum," in *Ancient Synagogues Revealed,* L.I. Levine, ed. Detroit: Wayne State University Press, 1982, pp. 57–59.

Loffreda, S., "The Late Chronology of the Synagogue at Capernaum," *IEJ* 23 (1973) 37–42.

——, "Reply to the Editor," *IEJ* 23 (1973) 184.

Additional Information About the Octagonal Church

Corbo, V., *The House of St. Peter at Capernaum.* Jerusalem: Franciscan Printing Press, 1969.
Strange, J.F. and Shanks, H., "Has the House Where Jesus Stayed in Capernaum Been Found?" *Biblical Archaeology Review* 8 (1982) 26–37.

Critical Evaluations of the Work of Corbo and Loffreda

North, R., "Discoveries at Capernaum," *Biblica* 58 (1977) 424–431.
Strange, J.F., "The Capernaum and Herodium Publications," *Bulletin of the American Schools of Oriental Research* 226 (1977) 65–73.

Additional Information About "Jewish Christianity"

Bagatti, B., *The Church from the Circumcision.* Jerusalem: Franciscan Printing Press, 1971.
Brown, R., "Not Jewish Christianity and Gentile Christianity But Types of Jewish/Gentile Christianity," *Catholic Biblical Quarterly* 45 (1983) 74–79.
Mancini, I., *Archaeological Discoveries Relative to the Judaeo-Christians.* Jerusalem: Franciscan Printing Press, 1971.

Chapter 6

The Synagogue

Avigad, N., "A Dated Lintel Inscription from the Ancient Synagogue of Nabratein," *Rabinowitz Bulletin* 3 (1960) 49–56. The author's decipherment of the inscription on the lintel, which was confirmed by the excavation of the synagogue.
Chiat, M.J.S., *Handbook of Synagogue Architecture.* Chico, Calif.: Scholars Press, 1982, pp. 41–45. A summary of archaeological discoveries at Nabratein with a bibliography.
Meyers, E.M., Strange, J.F. and Meyers, C.L., "Preliminary Report on the 1980 Excavations at en-Nabratein, Israel," *Bulletin of the American Schools of Oriental Research* 244 (1981) 1–26. This well-illustrated re-

port describes the results of the first season's work at Nabratein. A preliminary report on the second season and the final report on the project are forthcoming.

The Ark

Meyers, E.M., and Meyers, C.L., "Finders of a Real Lost Ark," *Biblical Archaeology Review* 7 (1981) 24–39. A popularly written explanation of the excavation of Nabratein, the finding of the ark and the significance of both.

Meyers, E.M., Strange, J.F. and Meyers, C.L., "The Ark of Nabratein—A First Glance," *Biblical Archeologist* 44 (1981) 237–243. An attempt by the excavators of Nabratein to describe the ark and its archaeological, cultural and religious context and significance.

Galilean Regionalism

Meyers, E.M., "Ancient Synagogues in Galilee: Their Religious and Cultural Setting," *Biblical Archeologist* 43 (1980) 97–108.

————, "The Cultural Setting of Galilee: The Case for Regionalism and Early Judaism," *Aufstieg und Niedergang der Römischen Welt* II.19.1, pp. 686–702.

————, "Galilean Regionalism as a Factor in Historical Reconstruction," *Bulletin of the American Schools of Oriental Research* 22 (1976) 93–101. These essays, by one of the principal excavators of Nabratein, show how archaeologists go about integrating their discoveries with those of literary historians in order to clarify the social and religious history of Galilee.

Post-Biblical Judaism and Early Christianity

Meyers, Eric M. and Strange, J.F., *Archaeology, the Rabbis and Early Christianity.* Nashville: Abingdon, 1981. A very valuable work illustrating how archaeology and historical literature are integrated in order to give a more complete and accurate description of the origins of both Judaism and Christianity.

Strange, J.F., "Archaeology and the Religion of Judaism in Palestine," *Aufstieg und Niedergang der Römischen Welt* II.19.1, pp. 646–685. Another of the principal excavators of Nabratein does a masterful job of integrating the vast amount of archaeological data from throughout Palestine which can aid our understanding of post-biblical Judaism.

This essay can help locate the significance of Nabratein against a wider background.

Chapter 7

Suggestions About the Future of Biblical Archaeology

Dever, William G., "Archaeological Method in Israel: A Continuing Revolution," *Biblical Archeologist* 43 (1980) 41–48.

———, "Archaeology," in the *Interpreter's Dictionary of the Bible,* Supplementary Volume, pp. 44–52.

———, *Archaeology and Biblical Studies: Retrospects and Prospects.* Evanston: Seabury-Western Theological Seminary, 1972.

———, "Biblical Archaeology or the Archaeology of Syria-Palestine?" *Christian News from Israel* 22 (1972) 21–23.

———, "Biblical Theology and Biblical Archaeology: An Appreciation of G. Ernest Wright," *Harvard Theological Review* 73 (1980) 1–15.

———, "The Impact of the 'New Archaeology' on Syro-Palestinian Archaeology," *Bulletin of the American Schools of Oriental Research* 242 (1981) 15–30.

For the views of other archaeologists on the future of biblical archaeology see the issues of the following journals, each of which devoted an entire number of the question of archaeology's future.

Biblical Archeologist 45 (Spring 1982) 73–108; 45 (Fall 1982) 201–228.

Bulletin of the American Schools of Oriental Research 242 (Spring 1981) 1–30.

Other Books in this Series

What are they saying about Mysticism? *by Harvey D. Egan, S.J.*

What are they saying about Christ and World Religions?
by Lucien Richard, O.M.I.

What are they saying about the Trinity? *by Joseph A. Bracken, S.J.*

What are they saying about non-Christian Faith?
by Denise Lardner Carmody

What are they saying about Christian-Jewish Relations?
by John T. Pawlikowski

What are they saying about the Resurrection? *by Gerald O'Collins*

What are they saying about Creation? *by Zachary Hayes, O.F.M.*

What are they saying about the Prophets? *by David P. Reid, SS.CC.*

What are they saying about Moral Norms? *by Richard M. Gula, S.S.*

What are they saying about Death and Christian Hope?
by Monika Hellwig

What are they saying about Sexual Morality? *by James P. Hanigan*

What are they saying about Jesus? *by Gerald O'Collins*

What are they saying about Dogma? *by William E. Reiser, S.J.*

What are they saying about Luke and Acts?
by Robert J. Karris, O.F.M.

What are they saying about Peace and War? *by Thomas A. Shannon*

What are they saying about Papal Primacy?
by J. Michael Miller, C.S.B.

What are they saying about Matthew? *by Donald Senior, C.P.*

What are they saying about the End of the World?
by Zachary Hayes, O.F.M.

What are they saying about Wisdom Literature?
by Dianne Bergant, C.S.A.